PHASES OF INDIA'S DEVELOPMENT: A LENSEYE VIEW

PHASES OF INDIA'S DEVELOPMENT: A LENSEYE VIEW

Dr. P.K. AGRAWAL, IAS (R)

PRINTS PUBLICATIONS PVT. LTD.
NEW DELHI

Published by :

Prints Publications Pvt. Ltd.
Prints House, 11, Darya Ganj
New Delhi - 110002
Phone: +91-11-45355555
E-mail : contact@printspublications.com
Website: www. printspublications.com

ISBN-978-81-927694-1-7

Published and Printed by Mr. Pranav Gupta on behalf of Prints Publications Pvt Ltd at Mohit Enterprises, Delhi

CONTENTS

JUDICIARY

LAND REFORM

GOOD GOVERNANCE

PREFACE

The book entitled "Phases of India's Development : A lenseye view" is a collection of my published columns and articles for the last four years in various magazines specially in the Bureaucracy Today. I am a regular column writer of the Bureaucracy Today which was for sometimes a fortnightly magazine.

Though the magazines generally cater to the current affairs yet I have dealt with current topics with permanent features, so that the book may be relevant for all times. The problems in the Indian polity reappear more or less on the same pattern.

I have an administrative background for about thirty six years in the field of taxation, general administration, land and seven years in the law practice. I have accordingly, divided the book under four sub-heads *i.e.* Bureaucracy, Judiciary, Land Reform and Good Governance. Land Reform has been my specialized field. I have got D.Phil in Land Reform laws of Uttar Pradesh and had worked for about eleven years in the Land and Land Reforms Department, Government of West Bengal on all important posts from bottom to the top. I strongly feel that land reform can solve most of the problems of poverty in India. However, India is a very vast, varied and complex country and none can vouch for to provide a complete solution. Some say that removal of poverty is the solution whereas the other say that industrialization in the age of globalization is the solution. Votaries of modern economics say that emphasis on education and health is the panacea. Some persons who claim to be expert on the Indian socio-political scenario put forward the idea that tackling corruption and delay in delivery of justice can solve all ills facing the country. However, all accept that the good governance is the main objective in whatever way it can be achieved. I have therefore, taken most of the viewpoints into consideration and come out with varied solutions after lot of research and personal experience including being on the other side of the government. All articles seek how welfare of people can be achieved.

Though my columns or articles written were of larger in size, yet I have included mostly the published ones so that reader is not burdened with unnecessary details. The reader of the modern internet era doesn't want to waste his time in digging the mine of knowledge. He wants readymade solution to the issue or matter in hand.

The sub heading wise approach can be summarized as follows;

BUREAUCRACY:

Bureaucracy is an inevitable institution. Therefore, there is need to get maximum output from this organization. It is a part of the executive of the state. However, political executives now-a-days also play crucial role. There is need to tackle irregularities and corruption patronized and perpetuated by them. Though a bureaucrat is not supposed to carry out the illegal orders of his superior officer, yet a poor bureaucrat cannot afford it on all occasions due to his insecurity of career and uncertainty of future.

The superior is supposed to confirm his oral instruction in writing subsequently. Bureaucrats are so well entrenched in rules and regulations that it is a difficult job to get the delivery of results by them. This is possible only when the superior officers or political executives lead them from front and by their good examples. Bureaucrats by their nature are generally indifferent and not accountable to public. They have to be oriented by training and motivation to the mission of the organization i.e.

welfare of people in case of government and earning of profit in public sector undertakings. Uninteresting work and lot of power have mode bureaucrats corrupt. The way out is to have expeditious decision-making so that bureaucrats can not organize bribery. Setting up of the institution of Ombudsman and setting up of special courts can help to tackle corruption among bureaucrats and political executives. Even U.N. is very keen to control corruption in the bureaucracy. There is need for civil service reforms. Recruitment should be based on transparent procedure and conduct of tests honestly. Transfers and postings should be done by independent civil service boards which is also directed by the Supreme Court of India. Bureaucrats should be governed by the Administrative Law so that they may follow proper procedure and know in advance, the consequences of infringement of such procedures or regulations. In USA even the President speaks the brief given by the bureaucrats. Police, being the part of bureaucratic set-up in India, should play proactive role to help developmental schemes rather than confining themselves only to apprehend thieves, dacoits, rapists or murderers. To discharge the onerous job of public welfare, the bureaucrats should be given a conducive environment of work, adequate pay and facilities but should also be accountable proportionate to the compensation received by them. However, bureaucrats should keep their good health and positive psychology suitable to perform their jobs effectively by doing yoga and pranayam as a suitable therapy for them. Computerisation or digitization of office is certainly a step forward but it should also be controlled so that grievances of the stake holders or public are redressed.

JUDICIARY:

Delay in disposal of cases is causing lot of worries to the people specially the litigants and set back to the galloping economy of India. The main cause of delay is frequent adjournments granted by the courts, tribunals and quasi-judicial bodies inspite of mandate in Order 17 Rule 1 of the Code of Civil Procedure that not more than three adjournments should be given to a party in a suit. One of the primary solutions is to increase the number of judges in all courts. The District and subordinate courts require more gearing up and supervision by their respective High Court. The Supreme Court has shown the way to liquidate pendency of cases by fixing of cases through the computer network, the grouping and classification of cases involving the similar question of law, the setting up of specialized Benches and the computerization of records. Alternative Dispute Resolution through arbitration, mediation, conciliation is the modern method to avoid regular long procedure of court cases. Mediation is a good method to settle consumer disputes amicably. Similarly, for the poor inmates languishing in prisons for a long time, free legal aid is the only solace.

LAND REFORM:

Implementation of land reform provides a bed-rock on which the palace of development can be built. China had achieved extra-ordinary progress and prosperity after giving land to its 90% landless people. So also Japan has successfully implemented land reforms. Distribution of government surplus land and recording of sharecropper on land are two main components of land reform apart from updating and computerization of land records. For this purpose, the landless persons have to be organized to claim their right of cultivation like in many countries in Africa, South America and South East Asia. It is a fact that factories cannot be built in sky. Land is required to set up factories. But minimum land should be acquired by the State for this purpose after giving proper opportunity of hearing to the affected persons and due compensation to them. The new Land Acquisition Act, 2013 is a revolutionary step which has provisions for social impact assessment provision of jobs to the affected persons and three to four times of market value of land as compensation to the affected land owners or families. Three articles on land reforms in Bangladesh, Pakistan and Nepal have been included so that India may know her neighbor countries well. With a good administrative approach, even the difficult job of land acquisition can be made simpler and within the target date. Delay in execution of projects costs government much more than the higher compensation awarded in the land acquisition of the project and subsequent litigation.

Removal of poverty is the aim of all land reform measures. Self-help groups (SHGs) can play a vital role. They can organize themselves into a group and do cultivation on the pattern of the Russian farming co-operatives without the intervention of the state machinery in their affairs. This is a pattern practiced successfully in Egypt and at few places in India.

GOOD GOVERNANCE:

Good governance is the mission of each state comprising of legislatures, executive and judiciary. The bureaucrats are the persons behind each legislation as they are experts in their field and put up the basic draft to Parliament or State Legislatures through Ministers who play double role. Therefore, the bureaucracy requires utmost attention. The executive should be honest, transparent, knowledgeable and prompt in their job. They should be easily accessible to people. The Public Grievance Machinery should be effective. Public has reverence towards their leaders who provide them good governance and keep on voting in their favour for years to come even in favour of their successors. Thrust areas of governance in India have been discussed critically viz. tackling Naxalism, the Ganga cleaning, skill development, taming black money, inter rivers-linking, Swachh Bharat Mission, CSR initiatives etc. Apart, some motivational articles are included like on utilizing weekends more fruitfully, more vital role played by the private sector and bureaucratization of private sector, performance of duties by the citizens and abhorrence of intolerance etc. The book Bhagwadgita is a great source of inspiration to the Indians. Excerpts from the Gita have been given to activate personnel to perform their duties. One miscellaneous article on the 'Freedom of India' has been included in the end which shows deep roots of democracy in India.

It is hoped that this consolidated work of mine will be welcome by administrators, political executives, judges, lawyers and public at large. It will specially useful for the candidates sitting in the competitive examinations for civil service. If some of the suggestions contained in the book are implemented, it will be my small contribution towards the nation building.

I thank the publishers of the magazines 'Bureaucracy Today', 'Business Economics', 'Rural Connect', 'Uday India' for re-publishing the columns and articles with some modification.

I also thank Mr. Pranav Gupta Director, Prints Publications Pvt. Ltd. for publishing this book.

Dr PK AGRAWAL

BUREAUCRACY

1

Anatomy of a Bureaucrat at Work

A bureaucrat is generally in permanent employment of the Government. He expects some measure of independence and autonomy, achievement and self-worth and a feeling of competence and being valued.

The personality of the bureaucrat is like the nature of an iceberg whose ninth tenth part is hidden within water. The bureaucrat is apt in the art of hiding his real personality. His decision, reaction and even mood have an impact on the well-being of society. He is an intelligent person who has the capacity to read the pulse of his stakeholders, mainly the public, and to respond suitably. In developing and less developed countries, bureaucrats are the cream of society. Even in developed countries, bureaucrats are socially well-recognized. Many young people in spite of high salaries in the private sector prefer to join Government or semi-Government organizations. These people, however, develop negativities after joining the Government because they have so many clients to oblige who have competitive demands and sometimes even rival demands Therefore, the brain of such a bureaucrat is a poor receptor of outside inputs, reflexes or light. As the whole society is his work field, he keeps his nose sensitive to smell rumours.

But the bureaucrat knows his limitations since his organization is very powerful as compared to him. He is just like a cog in a wheel. His boss is very insensitive to his suggestions.

Therefore, he wants to pose as if he has not received all the actionable information. He has big ears because he has an array of his assistants who are feeding him continuous information and giving their suggestions. But he doesn't keep his ears open to all the complaints because he knows well that he will not be able to act upon those complaints much less redress them because of the insensitive working of his office or organization. He tries to stop as many complaints reaching his ears as he can.

In such a scenario, the bureaucrat lives in contradictions. He desires something but does something else. He has not yet fully identified his personal goal with the mission of the organization. His personal needs or obligations are not finding full satisfaction in his job. His family obligations are not fulfilled. He has lot of peer pressure on him and pressure from his friends and relatives. As a result, the bureaucrat is not one in reality what he stands for himself. Or the bureaucrat poses himself what he is not from within. Thus he has a split personality full of contradictions. He finds difficulty in coping with occupational and personal hazards. The physical consequences of not being able to resolve a stressful situation directly by using our emergency resources can be very serious.

When the bureaucrat comes to his workplace free from stress, he deals with things with iron fist. He can take pleasant or unpleasant decisions consistent with his position or post in a bureaucratic organization. In the bureaucracy, firm decisions are expectedly backed by the power of sanction or reward or punishment with the decisionmaker. It is a fact that the bureaucrat has half-baked ideas as regards himself and even as regards the subject before him. He doesn't verify or update advances in society which have taken place after he entered the bureaucracy, firstly because he is occupied with day-to-day routine jobs and secondly, because he works in a closed .circuit. A bureaucrat is more opaque to new ideas or suggestions, firstly to hide his ignorance and secondly, due to his super ego.

In fact, in the bureaucracy, the decision is multilayer one. Sometimes it takes so much time in decision-making that the decision itself becomes irrelevant or redundant and is given up. On the other hand, when such kind of decision is notified, the section which initiated the file is sometimes itself surprised to find that the requirement was one thing whereas the decision finally arrived at is poles apart and it is difficult to correlate the two.

January, 16-31, 2015, Bureaucracy Today

♦♦♦

> *Good government only happens when the people working in it do their jobs, and do them well.*
>
> **— Matthew Lesko**

2

Psychology of a Bureaucrat

The bureaucrat is said to be the egoist person. Ego is the root of one's psychology. It creates an image of itself which puts one different from others. The ego defines one's personality and is a highly dynamic concept. It depends on factors of one's environment experience and will power. When a person joins the Government; he or she brings along experiences of his/her past. If a person comes from the lower middle class, he will be down to earth. A middle class bureaucrat knows his roots but tries to be in the upper class. Officers, who come from the economically middle class, constitute the bulk of the bureaucracy. They are the most vocal and represent the bureaucracy. Upper class bureaucrats maintain their class identity and are self-oriented and career minded from the beginning. They don't have much commitment to the job or to the mission of the organization. The economic characteristics of the Indian bureaucracy are those of the middle class. The pay, perks or status one gets in the bureaucracy except Class IV or "D" Group employees makes one to belong to the middle class.

The lower class or lower middle class and upper class bureaucrats have their rigid ideologies and thinking. They believe in free life and do not bind themselves with values. They compromise whenever opportunity is offered to them. It is the middle class whose psychology can be moulded according to the environment and its experiences. If the bureaucrat gets a good environment, he tries to put in his best. He has an urge to learn. He is the one who fights for the cause of the downtrodden in society and is basically patriotic and loyal. But he would like to keep his job security at all costs because he has nothing to fall back upon. If he has a sad experience during his early formation period of service by facing threats to his job, he will compromise with his principles in life. In any case either he will come out of his fiery test or will succumb to pressure or adverse situation.

As a result, his emotional balance breaks down and he becomes subject to disease and a burden to society. His will power is also formulated on the basis of his experience in the existing environment of-the bureaucratic organization. However, there are a few exceptions in every class who have well-firmed up will power or mission which does not get deviated under any adverse situation.

These people are the winner in the bureaucratic set-up. They develop the psychological identity of being the winner. They manage their emotions and the state of mind in areas where most people fail. For example, in the powerful bureaucratic set-up, one cannot have a frontal fight. One has to wait for chance and opportunity and then to strike with all powerful strokes. One has to slowly go up the ladder, sometimes compromising with the small things with a view to doing big things later on. In the case of interference or action by bureaucratic or political bosses, one has to accept the situation with a pinch of salt as part of professional hazards and then accumulate adequate capability to strike back positively.

One has to manage one's ego. An inflated ego often comes into conflict with other persons because in order to justify the volume of his ego, he claims credit for achievement which may be the result of hard work done by other people and not by him. At the same time, he denies responsibility for a failed action. The right-size ego can be developed by adopting the right attitude in life.

The middle class bureaucrat has to face lot of competition. It is this class which can change the reputation of a bureaucratic organization. The organization should have an objective appraisal system, a well-laid-down and declared transfer policy, an HR system, a motivational climate and basic physical facilities at the workplace. If these things are provided, not only will the bureaucratic organization achieve its mission but the bureaucrat also will have good psychology at home.

August 16–31, 2014, Bureaucracy Today

♦♦♦

Take up one idea. Make that one idea your life - think of it, dream of it, live on that idea. Let the brain, muscles, nerves, every part of your body, be full of that idea, and just leave every other idea alone. This is the way to success.

— Swami Vivekananda

3

Fear Psychosis among Bureaucrats

The Indian bureaucracy has become a green pasture for educated young persons because one gets an assured salary and an assurance for a reasonably good living even after retirement.- Therefore, there is lot of social conflict due to reservation in Government jobs either overtly or covertly.

The protagonists of reservation for minorities argue that due representation to the minorities in Government jobs is itself an achievement. Let the long period of injustice to the minorities be first undone and only then an objective analysis can follow.

Similarly, gender equality is nowadays an accepted fundamental principle of the polity. There is equality between men and women. Initially, women were more represented in routine low jobs. But now there is increasing emphasis on women representation in all types of jobs. Time is coming when female bosses will be visible more than male bosses.

A bureaucrat has to function within conflicting claims and counter-claims. A poor bureaucrat, therefore, feels being cornered or not welcomed at his workplace. This creates psychological barriers in his job and insecurity of his job looms large in his mind creating mental and physical disorders. If he has a superior officer who is biased against him in the societal set-up, he will not be liked by his boss. Similarly, if he is superior caste-wise or status-wise in his societal set-up, he will look down upon his boss when he meets him. Likewise, male workers may have a superior complex vis- a-vis their female bosses. But

Weber's bureaucratic organization is such that there is no place for all such feelings or emotions. If any action is not warranted by norms of the organization, it will be treated as an act of indiscipline and the bureaucrat will be accountable for his unbecoming behaviour.

Reservation for women, up to 50% of the Government posts has been held valid for female candidates in India by the apex court in various judgments as Article 15(3) of the Constitution provides for a special provision for women and children. Similarly, the reservation of certain posts exclusively for women is valid under Article 15(3). In the same vein, to ameliorate the conditions of women in India, the Supreme Court laid down in its Visakha case judgment that sexual harassment of working women amounts to a violation of the rights guaranteed by the right to equality and dignity. In this case the court issued detailed guidelines/directions on the subject which were implemented by the Government in public and private organizations with more sanctity and sincerity than the implementation of a statute. These guidelines were issued after the incident of brutal gangrape of a social worker in Rajasthan. The Government of India subsequently got passed the Sexual Harassment of Women at Work Place (Prevention, Prohibition and Redressal) Act, 2013 on the same lines which is being implemented throughout the country. The Act enjoins upon every employer to provide a safe working environment at the workplace for women.

There is so much innovation and diversification in the jobs performed by bureaucrats that the old guard feel sometimes lost. They require lot of training and retraining and that is also not always available at their workplace. An innovation to tone up the sagging working of the bureaucracy is the application of Computer Technology extensively in governance to make it faster, more objective and more transparent. The objective of electronic governance, in the Government's view, goes far beyond mere computerization of standalone back-office operations. It is not about hardware and software but marks a fundamental change in the way the Government operates and interacts with citizens.

Bureaucrats find it difficult to learn new innovations very fast. This creates psychological problem in their personal life and is reflected in their working. As far as it can be lessened, it is better for the governmental system.

February 1-15, 2015, Bureaucracy Today

♦♦♦

All our dreams can come true, if we have the courage to pursue them.

— Walt Disney

4

Mega Bureaucracy of Central Government

As the Government of India is a large bureaucracy, it is very powerful and is indifferent, neutral and inaccessible. It runs on the prescribed rules and regulations which are made for people. However, the size of the public bureaucracy is not increasing as per an increase in population. The Central bureaucracy is so big in size that one fails to trace one's invisible boss who ultimately takes decisions. Therefore, the functioning of the Union Government depends on the self-motivation of an employee. Most people say that the Central Government is run by a few employees in each department. A motivated employee performs his or her duty and even works for others who are lazy and work shirkers.

In the Central Government, the top bureaucrat i.e. the Secretary is very powerful and it is very difficult to reverse his decision. His decision is based on many layers and hierarchies in the bureaucracy, sometimes including the approval of a Minister before it is made public. The Secretary is not supposed to send most of the files to his Minister. He represents the Government as far as the rules of business and the Constitution of India are concerned and he is accountable to the public as well as to Parliamentary Sub-committees. When the same bureaucrat succumbs to the dictates of his political masters, an illegal chain of decisions starts and the work hierarchy is disturbed. Two such incidents known as the 2G scam and the Coalgate scam respectively in the years 2012 and 2014 came to light in which a few lakh crores of rupees or millions of dollars were allegedly mishandled by the nexus of politicians/ Ministers and senior bureaucrats. The beneficiaries greased the palms of lower level officials and got away with the booty. In these two scams, and in a few more cases, some bureaucrats were involved in criminal proceedings for bribery and corrupt practices even after their retirement.

This is not accepted by other bureaucrats since many innocent senior officers, in their opinion were named in FIRs by the CBI. At many places, the CBI and even higher courts could not appreciate the manner of bureaucratic functioning to boost the sagging economy at the relevant time by giving concessions to private sector businessmen on their terms and conditions. As a result, the most senior bureaucrats, who were on the verge of their retirement, stopped taking decisions during the UPA-II regime from the year 2012 to nearly 2014. This paralysis of the decision-making process by the bureaucrats caused the defeat of the UPA-II Government in the 2014 Lok Sabha elections. Prime Minister Narendra Modi after assuming office reassured the bureaucrats of service security if they delivered the results.

However, it is not understandable how effectively and practically his campaign to protect bureaucrats from the vagaries of inquiries, media accusations or media trial and a subsequent onslaught on their personal life even after retirement will be successful. The actions by Central Government bureaucrats are subject to scrutiny by courts, the Comptroller and Auditor General of India and Parliament. This further inhibits their taking fast decisions. A person with so many masters is often a confused man. Therefore, they being the true representatives of the Weber bureaucracy should be properly governed by a definite body of clear and unambiguous rules and regulations under valid Acts and the umbrella of the code of conduct.

The code of conduct is required to be rewritten for officers in the light of the fast moving age of information technology, globalization and economic and social developments, especially in the case of the large-size bureaucracy of the Government of India which cannot be reached personally.

June 16–30, 2015, Bureaucracy Today

◆◆◆

5

Problems of Bureaucracy in Uttar Pradesh

The State of Uttar Pradesh is bigger than many of the countries in the World, both in respect of area and population. The bureaucracy of Uttar Pradesh is also of mega size and is a very powerful one.

After Independence, political instability started in UP in 1967. From 1967 to 1997, there were 18 Chief Ministers and four spells of President's rule. Accordingly, cracks started appearing in the IAS collectively. Loyalties kept on shifting and officers gradually began to be identified with different political parties, factions or individuals. At times politicians and civil servants became ungrudging partners in manipulative and shady deals.

After 1967, UP politicians were not having a broad vision like the ones who participated in the freedom struggle. They developed self-aggrandizement and corruption crept into the rank and file. Political executives found an easy way to make money through transfers of officers and staff. Thus, transfer became an industry in UP. It is estimated that during six years, 1991-1997, over 3,000 IAS/IPS officers were transferred. There was no transfer policy. The formal system of transfer was in a shambles which was kept as such by senior bureaucrats and political executives to serve their vested interests. Most of the transfers were dictated from the Chief Minister's Office. In a large number of cases, the Chief Secretary was not even consulted. In as many as 37 districts, tenures of Collectors varied from 12 months to 18 months. In 13 districts the tenures were between 18 and 24 months; in 11 districts they were between six and nine months and in three districts they were between three and six months. In another three districts the periods of postings on an average were three months or less.

The Supreme Court judgment in the case of former *UP Chief Secretary T.S.R. Subramanian & Ors* Vs *Union of India & Ors* is being flagrantly violated in the State. The judgment was dated October 31, 2013 (Civil Writ Petition No. 82 of 2011).

The apex court directed inter alia that the views of the Chief Secretary can only be overruled by the political executive by recording reasons: a Civil Service Board be constituted within a period of three months with high-ranking service officers, and there is necessity of minimum tenure to ensure efficient service delivery and also increased efficiency.

A study of responses from IAS officers reveals that they assign high value to improving their skills and capabilities, greater decentralization and delegation of authority, reduced political interference and clearly defined performance-reward linkages. On the other hand, they assign low value to risk taking and drastic changes in the system. The external assessment of IAS officers is that they project themselves as experts on most things, and are arrogant, shrewd, manipulative and procedure and rule-focused. However, the IAS Officers Association in UP had rightly begun the purge by voting two former Chief Secretaries among the most corrupt officers.

The position of lower level bureaucracies is more degraded. Most of the UP Government officers, engineers, doctors, inspectors and clerks are considered corrupt. Observers say the UP Police is thoroughly corrupt. Informed sources say corruption is even well entrenched in the judiciary of UP. As a result, industries have migrated from UP. Time is not far off when industries will leave Noida and Ghaziabad if the present state of administrative affairs is not improved.

It seems that the people of UP have started looking beyond caste, creed or religion and are eyeing development of the State as the sole factor of assessing the Government's performance. It is hoped that the people's aspirations will ultimately be reflected directly through their elected representatives and will percolate down gradually to the lowest level of the bureaucracy.

June 1–15, 2015, Bureaucracy Today

♦♦♦

> *Problems are not stop signs, they are guidelines.*
>
> **– Robert H. Schuller**

6

Ideal Bureaucrats of Gujarat

After Independence, statutes were enacted to introduce the Panchayat system of decentralized administration in Indian States. The bureaucracy of many State Governments did not cooperate in connivance with political executives to wield unhindered power by them. But the bureaucracy of Gujarat helped to grow up co-operative societies like milk cooperatives such as Amul and Panchayati Raj institutions both in letter and in spirit since the beginning which was done by West Bengal and Kerala in the year 1978 after the Left Front Governments came to power with thumping majorities there.

However, Maharashtra is another neighbouring State which has closely followed in the footsteps of Gujarat. Gujarat is a well-administered State and has been the first choice of new entrants to the IAS who believe in good governance. It is a pleasure to interact with a general public servant in Gujarat who is very responsive and helpful unlike public servants elsewhere in the country. This is one of the reasons why Gujarat has made unprecedented progress in India and people from all other States are flocking to Gujarat for jobs. Gujarat has attracted maximum foreign direct investment (FDI). The country is now watching whether Prime Minister Narendra Modi can implement the Gujarat model of progress in other parts of India which are plagued with the lack of motivation, excessive dependence on government grants and the lack of work culture.

In Gujarat Government offices, clerks do not go to get files approved by officers which should be normally done by them.

Everybody takes proper and quick decision at his/ her level or pushes the file upward. There are not many complaints by bureaucrats of political interference or undue pressure. As a result, there have been tremendous outstanding achievements by individual bureaucrats in their respective fields and the State in general. Political executives have traditionally provided freedom to bureaucrats to function and for experiments. They have maintained their faith in bureaucrats. The level of integrity among Gujarat bureaucrats is one of the highest in India. The bureaucrats made the dirtiest Gujarat cities like Surat the cleanest cities. The dirtiest Sabarmati has been made the cleanest river in India. Business has increased manifold and the per capita income in Gujarat is now one of the highest in the country. Electricity, water supply, education and health facilities have reached every village and industries are scattered all over the State without any exception. Tribal villages in Gujarat now have 24-hour electricity and safe drinking water. Irrigation water from the Sardar Sarovar Dam has reached all nooks and corners of Gujarat. Even the areas of Rann of Kutch and the district of Bhuj which were chronically known for the shortage of water have now plenty of drinking water.

The story of Gujarat is bright because the bureaucrats and local population work hand-in-hand. The local population has the culture to be self-dependent. NGOs and local charitable organizations are so well spread, equipped and resourceful that Government agencies have only to play a secondary role in normal times as well as during emergency situations. For this, Gujaratis settled abroad are to be thanked because they send lot of remittances of their hard-earned dollars. I am sure that Gujarat is providing us some thoughts to ponder over.

May 16–31, 2015, Bureaucracy Today

♦♦♦

7

Ring is Buzzing without Reply

The bureaucracy is a closed world and runs on formal rules and regulations. During a long period of its functioning, the bureaucracy loses track of its mission or goal and the observance of rules becomes its sole object. This is the most soothing environment for work for bureaucrats as none can challenge them in their field.

The elected representatives of people come with some mandate to perform mainly to deliver public welfare measures. If the matter is left entirely to bureaucrats, they will take unusually long time to implement those measures which cannot be permitted, especially in this fast moving world of Information Technology and Internet.

The common man faces lot of problems with government or semi-government bodies or private companies employed by the government for public functioning. Every organization is supposed to have a public grievances redressal system to meet the demands of consumers or stakeholders. This is not managed well. Then stakeholders or members of the public try to contact higher officers in the bureaucracy. But they are not adequately responsive because of two reasons. Firstly, the superior officer may not be well conversant with the way his organization is run by his subordinates. Secondly, he may be showing indulgence towards his subordinates with a fear of their unpleasant reaction or he may be involved with them to keep the organization inefficient to perpetuate his hegemony or to indulge in corruption.

When a person receives no reply on his petition, he runs here and there to find action on his file. He then searches the website of the Ministry, department or the office concerned as he cannot meet the head of the office easily. If at all he gets the date of appointment, it will be quite late. By the time, the purpose of his petition is defeated. The general mode of quick contact is through dialling telephones or mobile numbers displayed on the website or in front of the office. Unfortunately, most of these contact numbers are not available as these are not updated.

If one finds a valid contact number, it is difficult to get a proper reply. The Private Secretary of a senior bureaucrat will say that *Sahab* is not available. He has left for a meeting or is on a tour or is on leave. Though the Private Secretary can redress most of the public grievances, he will generally not take the risk to sort out problems. Thus public resentment increases and is reflected during elections when people vote against the establishment.

There can be a way out. A common telephone number can be assigned to a government office where a phone operator may not help redress a public grievance or give information sought but can come back to the complainant with information within 24 hours whatever is available in whatever raw form. This will be like a consumer helpline in vogue. Most of the complainants are information seekers and they will be happy even if the decision goes against them like in court cases. Most of them will be happy to know that their petitions are being processed whatever way it be. Alternatively, every officer may be instructed to keep half an hour free to reply to public calls by government notification.

Bureaucrats who are open to telephonic calls from selected persons will be encouraging middle men in their decision-making for ulterior purposes. It is a fact that an officer who picks up phone calls himself is well informed how his office functions and can take corrective measures to improve efficiency in his office. A public officer is a link between the public and his office.

He belongs to the public domain and his expenses of phone and mobile calls are met by public revenue. He is thus duty bound to reply to public calls.

June 16–30, 2016, Bureaucracy Today

◆◆◆

> *Spread love everywhere you go. Let no one ever come to you without leaving happier.*
>
> **— Mother Teresa**

8

Obeying Illegal Orders of Superior Officer is not a Defence

The story begins after the Second World War when under Herr Hitler, millions of war crimes were committed by massacring the people. To try those persons responsible, the Nuremberg trials were held in Germany. Hitler's deputy Hermann Goering a close confidant of Hitler pleaded that he had simply obeyed the orders of his Commander-in-Chief. This plea was not accepted by the Judges.

On October, 1946, twelve high ranking Nazis were sentenced to death in a landmark judgment by the International War Crimes Tribunal in Nuremberg. Among those condemned to death by hanging were Joachim Von Ribbentrop, Nazi Minister of foreign affairs. It was held that subordinate is bound to obey lawful order of superior only. Respondeat Superior *i.e.* Let the Superior be responsible is not an admissible defence.

This principle in the criminal law was adopted from the common law doctrine. As per doctrine of Vicarious Responsibility in law of Tort, a master is liable for the wrong of a servant. Specifically the doctrine makes an employer or principal liable for the wrong of an employee or agent if it was committed within the scope of his employment or agency (Perdue Vs Mitchall).

The person deciding an unlawful act to be done by his servant or agent is answerable as if he had done the act with his own hand. (Knott Vs. London Country Council 1934, KB 126)

The Nuremberg charter clearly lays down that it is illegal to follow the order to commit a war crime in utter violation of human rights and accordingly the person by committing war crimes will be held responsible for his actions irrespective of the fact that he was asked by the superior officer to do those highhandedness or illegal acts. However, they were given the fair trial. Remaining cases of Nuremberg trials are still going on.

Similarly, there was a Tokyo Trial for the war crimes committed mostly by the Japanese against the Chinese after the post World War II which has been published in 80 volumes, nearly 50,000 pages by the Shanghai Jiao Tong University Press that also reiterated the principal laid down in the Nuremberg trials.

The similar situation arose in India to try the persons responsible for excesses done during emergency under the Prime Minister Late Mrs. Indira Gandhi by Justice Shah Commission. The Shah Commission after hearing the perpetrators of excesses during emergency gave a report.

Shah Commission suggested to take stringent actions against those bureaucrats who committed excesses beyond the call of their duties which further demoralized the already fragmented bureaucracy.

Shri V. C Shukla & others were held guilty. Shri Shukla held key portfolios in the Union Govt, including Communications, Parliamentary Affairs, Water Resource and External Affairs. He was a propagandist as information and Broadcasting Minister during the Emergency days and imposed the media censor policy during that period when freedom of speech was under attack. Mr. Shukla stood by his decision and owned them before the Shah Commission. Similarly many other officers were held liable and were punished. Their service careers were—adversely affected. The finding of the Shah Commission report has found echo in various judgments of the Supreme Court later on.

The Supreme Court held that the prolonged detention of the Petitioner even after his acquittal was wholly unjustified and illegal. (Rudul Shah V. State of Bihar (AIR 1983 SC 1086, (1983) 4 SCC 141). The Hon'ble Supreme Court further maintained that crime is against the society and "a crime never dies."

The doctrine of sovereign immunity *i.e.* King can do no wrong is not available when the State or its officers acting in the course of employment infringe a person's fundamental right of life and personal liberty as guaranteed by Article 21 of the Constitution of India.

Section 166 of the Indian Penal Code clearly lays down that "Whoever, being a public servant, knowingly disobeys any direction of the law as to the way in which he is to conduct himself as such public servant, intending to cause, or knowing it to be likely that he will, by such disobedience, cause injury to any person, shall be punished with simple imprisonment for a term which may extend to one year, or with fine, or with both."

There is no exception that he will be protected if he follows the orders of his superior officer.

On the contrary, the superior public servant will be liable for illegal acts of the subordinates which is his duty as superior officer.

He can be punished if offence is committed with one half of the maximum punishment *i.e.* longest terms of such imprisonment or with such fine as is provided for that offence or with both. If the offence or illegal act is not committed, the punishment may extend to one fourth of the longest term or with fine provided for the offence or with both (Section 119 of the I. P. C.).

The founding fathers dreamt that they were laying the foundation of a public spirited public service for independent India. A civil servant has to combine the qualities of a king, who pleases his subjects by doing their welfare and the wisdom of a saint. The combination of the two *i.e.* power, efficiency, professionalism and energy to work will enable him to perform his duties to achieve welfare of people.

All India services personnel which have the shield and the security given to them by the Constitution of India should be sufficient to take a firm stand where such action is called for.

It is thus the duty and professional ethics of every bureaucrat that he should follow only the legal orders or lawful orders of his superior officers. In case of pressure on him, he should clearly mention with cogent reasons that he defers with the Superior officer and the order of the Superior officer is being implemented because it his duty to issue orders of the government.

However, public will know orders issued in his name but internally and actually he has simply carried out the illegal, unlawful and unjustified orders of his invisible superior officer who are generally political executives in India. Ultimately 'Dharma' protects. 'Dharma' according to Gandhiji is the voice of one's conscience and according to Buddha, it is the righteous action which speaks through the constitution and law in the present age.

December, 2013, Just Bureaucracy

♦♦♦

9

The Superior should Confirm Oral Instructions in Writing

There has been a long debate whether the subordinate should obey the oral instructions of administrative superiors. The famous Nurembuerg Trial Tribunal after the Second World War held that the oral instruction if illegal should not be acted upon. However, the Army cannot act on this arrangement but now these orders can be recorded on magnetic tape even in the battlefield.

The golden maxim had been incorporated in the All India Services (Conduct) Rules, 1968 for IAS officers and others. But it has been followed more in breach than in observance. Whenever any subordinate officer requests a superior officer to confirm his oral orders in writing, the superior officer generally feels offended. He tries to cow down the subordinate in many other ways if he has to confirm all his oral orders in writing. As a result, the subordinate officer starts trembling and loses his peace of mind. The political superior generally says that he issues illegal oral orders when he is away from the office on official tour or otherwise. However, his private secretary can confirm his orders in writing in office. Whenever the subordinate official puts the file for confirmation, the file is kept pending for months increasing the anxiety and insecurity of the subordinate day by day. But this is one of the ways to prevent corruption and inefficiency in the bureaucratic set-up which is eating away its vitals.

This issue of public interest was for the first time elaborately adjudicated upon and finally was made law of the land by the Supreme Court of India in the *TSR Subramanian & Ors Vs Union of India & Ors* case on October 31, 2013. The apex court lays down:

"The civil servants cannot function on the basis of verbal or oral instructions, orders, suggestions, propasals, etc., and they must also be protected against wrongful pressure exerted by the administrative superiors, political executive, business and other vested interests. There must be some record to demonstrate how the civil servant has acted, if the decision is not his but he is acting on the oral directions, instructions. He should record such instructions in the file."

It is more essential nowadays because the citizens have the rights guaranteed under Section 3 of the Right to Information Act, 2005. Rule 3 (3) (iii) of the All India Services (Conduct) Rules specifically requires that all orders from superior officers to record shall ordinarily be in writing. Where in exceptional circumstances action has to be taken on the basis of oral directions, it is mandatory for the superior officer to record the same in writing. If the Minister is not available, his private secretary should confirm his verbal or telephonic order in writing in his absence immediately.

The highest court of the country has directed all the State Governments and Union Territory Administrations to issue directions like Rule 3(3) of the All India Service (Conduct) Rules, 1968, in their respective States and UTs which will be carried out within three months from October 31, 2013. Before the date of judgment, the AIS (Conduct) Rule was optional but the same has become now law. Everybody in India is supposed to follow it. More than a year has elapsed but most of the government or semi-government bodies or local self-government units have not implemented this solemn order of the Supreme Court. Does it augur well for our democratic polity?

It is specially observed in panchayats and municipal bodies that elected executives exert undue influence on their officers to obey their irregular verbal orders to enrich their men and themselves and make law-abiding officers indefensible. As a result, they succumb to such unhealthy tactics and pressures and a chain of corruption starts, at the cost of the public exchequer.

If there are government instructions in compliance with the Supreme Court's order, the rule-abiding bureaucrats will have at least readymade defence of such a circular. Thus, recording of oral instructions or directions is necessary for fixing responsibility and ensure accountability in the functioning of civil servants.

December 16–31, 2014, Bureaucracy Today

♦♦♦

The most elementary qualification demanded of a minister is honesty and incorruptibility. It is, in addition, necessary not only that he should possess this qualification but also that he should appear to possess it.

— Sir Ivor Jennings

10

Postings should not be Based on Confidential Reports alone

At present, most of the administrative postings are based on confidential reports which are given partly on subjective considerations in spite of guidelines to be objective. To please one's boss, one has to be docile, obedient and to the liking of the boss. It is said that IAS officers in India are not scared of *'Sher'* (Lion) but are scared of CAR *i.e.* confidential annual report. Thus, from the beginning of his career, an official learns to compromise in his working and tries to build an aura around himself that he is being liked by everybody in the organization. Naturally people in a bureaucratic organization do not like to implement lots of reforms and innovations as these create disturbances in otherwise seemingly calm waters. As a result, in India we have created only middle class or lower middle class organizations as regards their efficiency in the Government as well as in the private sector.

In the present age of globalization, we require fast-moving organizations and their personnel at least at the helm of their affairs should be quick decision takers otherwise these organizations will become redundant and obsolete and will be left behind in the race of progress.

It is observed that honest and compromising officials go up the ladder in the administrative set-up in our country. As a result, we have mostly the indecisive and indifferent personnel or officers at the top. They wait for the nod or instructions from their political executives who neither have the vision nor the capacity to lead except in exceptional cases to take India ahead in the 21st century. The political executives are more concerned about looking after their constituencies, their political parties and their own self-interest and delivering the booty to their supporters indirectly through the "spoils system" as prevalent in the US. In this adverse scenario, the administrative head has to stand up to the challenge against the negative approach at the top and below. It is right that honest and normal working personnel are also given their promotions in turn along with fast moving personnel but they are not placed in key posts where continuous directions have to emerge as per law keeping pace with the changing times so as to keep the economy growing and law and order and corruption in check.

It is seen that the Centre and most of the State Governments adopt soft options and go in for non-controversial and honest officers. Therefore India is known as a "soft State" around the World. The administration is not meant to promote honesty by not taking decisions. Integrity is the basic requirement or tenet of a bureaucrat. The administration has a mission to accomplish to ensure the welfare of citizens, access to land and food security in rural areas and the availability of jobs, electricity and water in urban areas along with a non-discriminatory regulatory administrative structure. An official or officer is subservient to the mission or the election manifesto of the ruling political party but not to the whims of its ministers or elected representatives provided the mission conforms to the Constitution of India and laws and statutes in force.

Thus the confidential report should invariably focus on the positive achievements of an official or officer other than "no complaint" or "no conflict" report.

In the overenthusiasm of taking decisions, the official or officer should not become arbitrary, despot, autocrat or dictator. He or she has to ensure that the decision making process is guided by the welfare of people for all sections of society speedily. Therefore side by side an anti-corruption mechanism has to be in place which also watches the fast decision makers on a day-to-day basis.

The time is ripe when we require a political and administrative leadership who can have foresight and can take hard decisions which may not even find favour with the media which works primarily for the commercial interests of their mentors or owners. It is also for the Hon'ble Courts to give due leverage and scope to executives to function freely in their domain rather than indirectly reviewing their each and every major decision at the behest of some learned lawyers who have more paper experience than field experience. Executives go through the rigma-role of day-to-day life more than any other organ of the State. Of course, their actions are always subject to review by legislatures and even by the courts of law if they misuse their power and authority to the detriment of the teeming millions.

June 1–15, 2014, Bureaucracy Today

◆◆◆

> *In a hierarchy every employee tends to rise to his level of incompetence.*
>
> **– The Peter Principle**

11

Why Retirement at 60?

India is craving for the creation of jobs. Life expectancy in India has considerably increased due to good work done in the health and social security spheres by successive Governments in the country. But retirement in the bureaucratic set-up is still either at 58 years of age or maximum at 60 years of age. When one is physically fit and mentally alert at the year of 60 years, one naturally looks for a job to keep oneself busy and to continue to contribute to society. A person at the age of 60 years has lot of experience with him. Therefore his retirement at 60 will be detrimental to the interests of society.

An officer at the age of 60 years is generally at the helm of affairs in the executive wing of the state. Top and important decisions flow down through him. He has the manoeuvring powers of taking important decisions. Since he has zero work after his busiest schedule, he looks for a job after retirement. Political executives or top bureaucratic persons are happy to oblige him. Thus an unhealthy or a wrong decision-making process flows from the top to the bottom.

It is a fact that it is very difficult to catch the retiring senior bureaucrats into the net of vigilance or departmental proceedings. In the present dilatory system of government functioning,the decision will be finalized against them after four years when their past actions cannot be reopened or challenged as per Conduct Rules as the incumbents also tend to forget and as per rules are to be given proper opportunity of hearing-before any punishment. The availability of pension makes a government servant better placed than his counterpart in the private sector. It was observed during the UPA-II Central

Government that the retiring Secretaries did not take any decisions because the CBI sword was hanging over them to review all their actions. A bureaucrat works for pension during his whole period of service. He would not like to take any risk whatsoever.

A fine balance has to be struck. As far as possible, serving bureaucrats should be posted in all regulatory bodies and as arbitrators because they have higher accountability. The retired bureaucrats may be posted mostly in commissions where there is more requirements of reading, counseling and patience. But in no case the time taken by a commission should be increased like an unending tail which happened with most of the commissions like the Ayodhya Commission.

However, the meritorious among the retired bureaucrats can be tried on important posts but not at the cost of demoralization of the serving bureaucrats. The retired bureaucrats may be taken by political parties by getting them elected on their ticket and then making them ministers. Then they will perform better. In times to come, the latter route will be more popular as the public at large is fast losing its faith in politicians. However, this is also bad for democracy The need is, therefore, to have an independent, fast and impartial vigilance set-up to bring the guilty public servants to book and take exemplary action against the corrupt and the crook whosoever they are and howsoever big they may be.

This approach with some modification will hold well in respect of the private sector in India too.

1–15 Sept. 2014, Bureaucracy Today

◆◆◆

> *No government ever voluntarily reduces itself in size. Government programs, once launched, never disappear.*
>
> **— Ronald Reagen**

12

Corruption among Bureaucrats

Corruption and bureaucrats are closely interlinked. With regard to a bureaucrat or public servant, corruption means and includes the habitual acceptance of gratification, the receipt of any valuable thing without consideration, the misappropriation of government funds, the abuse of one's official position to obtain pecuniary advantage and the possession of pecuniary resources or property in excess of one's known sources of income.

CAUSES OF GRAFT

Bureaucrats indulge in corruption due to several reasons. Bureaucrats are offered speed money to expedite their decisions or to push up files to avoid delays if no harm is caused to the Government's interests.

Bribe is given to exercise discretion by a bureaucrat in favour of a private person as per law or rules. This refers to widespread corruption in various quasi-judicial authorities and government agencies where bureaucrats without rules or guidelines being prescribed can exercise their discretion.

There are bureaucrats who get government jobs after paying a bribe. There are others who from the beginning decide to go in for corruption as it will give them status in society. Corruption is rooted in acquisitive or artificial society where the status of individuals and the position of their families are judged by what they possess rather than by what they are. The acquisition of wealth has become sine qua non of life. People indulge in acquiring wealth without caring for the means they adopt.

Few bureaucrats find that indulging in corruption is a beneficial adventure from the cost-benefit analysis. People try to get rid of charges of corruption by spending ill-earned money on hiring reputed lawyers. Thus they save surplus money to have stylist and good life even after retirement in addition to pension available for government jobs.

There is lot of security provided in government jobs. Therefore, overassurance to bureaucrat impels them to go in for such adventure of corruption.

TACKLING CORRUPTION

Corruption cannot be tackled without co-operation from bureaucrats. There is a majority of bureaucrats who are in favour of weeding out corruption but they are shy of coming forward in support of the campaign as the power of corrupt bureaucrats is writ large. Corruption has to be tackled through sustained efforts by the bureaucracy or civil service.

In the US, the salaries of bureaucrats nowadays are on a par with private sector earnings. As a result, bureaucrats who wield so much power do not feel themselves inferior to their counterparts in the private sector in a society in which pay is one of the indicators of status symbol.

Civil servants are asked to take decisions in matters where there is no conflict of interest. The Governments of most developed countries forbid civil servants from involvement in taking decisions in which they have financial interests. In most cases, both bureaucrats and top political appointees must disclose their financial assets to a public agency earmarked by the Government.

To speed up a genuine disposal of routine files like those on paying taxes or fees, the public doesn't see corruption as endangering the system as the customer or the public itself is interested in taking advantage out of turn. So the efforts by the private citizens to tempt government officials to accept bribe should be equally punishable which has not been done in many countries. India has happily done this by bringing change in law.

The French and Canadian solutions focus more on administrative than criminal remedies. In Italy, strong anti-corruption measures are in practice. As a consequence, bureaucrats there have slowed down the decision-making process. This is more harmful for the polity. Government business and the economy should move fast. If required, the commission of questionable acts should include indecision or delay in decision-making as amounting to corruption. In law, commission and omission are the two sides of the same coin.

1–15, July, 2015, Bureaucracy Today

♦♦♦

> *The World is my country, all mankind are my brethren, and to do good is my religion.*
>
> **—Thomas Paine**

13

Corruption Creates Imbalance in the Economy

The Supreme Court of India in many cases has observed that corruption is not only a punishable offence but it also undermines human rights indirectly and systematic corruption is a human rights violation in itself as it leads to systematic economic crisis *(State of Maharashtra & CBI Vs Balakrishna Dattatrye Kumbhar)*. In another case, the apex court held that the accused is presumed to be corrupt till he is exonerated either by the Appellate court or the Revisional court *(Lily Thomas case, 2013, SC)*. The court further held that corruption is a serious malady undermining the very health of the polity. Trial, therefore, in corruption cases is to be conducted speedily within a year from the date of framing charges. Let the case of corruption be put on fast track.

Following the Supreme Court observations in various cases Justice A V Chandrashekara of the High Court of Karnataka while rejecting the bail plea of Ms Jayalalitha, the then Chief Minister of Tamil Nadu, held on October 7, 2014 that the lower court has applied its mind in the case of acquisition of disproportionate assets by her to the tune of Rs 66.65 crore during her Chief Ministership from June 24, 1991 to May 13, 1996. In fact, her case amply proves how the corrupt money was used in non-productive purposes as she had amassed seven kilograms of gold and jewellery. She had a record number of *sarees* and *chappals* and had spent lavishly on the wedding of her foster son, Sudhakaran, and was jailed along with her friend and Sudhakaran. The wedding of Sudhakaran had prompted many other businessmen and industrialists to organize similar weddings, including a steel tycoon who spent around Rs 350 crore on the marriage of his son, though now divorced. Such types of ostentatious expenditure only pulls back the country's economy and the common citizen feels deprived of, thereby violating his human rights.

The amount which was found in excess of Jayalalitha's accounted income was from 32 companies or business enterprises which actually didn't perform any worthwhile productive activity. With this huge wealth acquired by Jayalalitha during 1991-1996, about 30 small factories of textile, garment, yarn or paper manufacturing could have been started providing livelihood to more than 1,000 families.

Similarly, the tycoon could have opened a small steel factory or made a coal mine operational in his native State, West Bengal, ensuring direct livelihood to about 1,000 families and indirectly benefiting many thousand people of India by giving fillip to the Indian economy.

Money is more intoxicating than wine. Black money is parked in foreign countries which preach transparency and integrity to the developing nations but give shelter to corruption without any reservations or shame. When there is pressure to unearth this money, it travels back to the country of its origin in the form of foreign equity or is spent during elections or is, invested in the real estate sector or in Bollywood. When it is invested back, it heats up the economy. There is a price hike in the sector in which it is invested and there is general damage to the economy.

Black money can also voluntarily be disclosed as per government schemes from time to time. Those having black money can pay the highest rate of income tax along with penalty. Its tentacles are otherwise so powerful that even the powers and resources of the Government cannot tame it. It doesn't mean that the Government should surrender. At the same time black money holders should regain their conscience. They should correct their mistakes and put their black money into the useful development sectors of the country's economy directly or indirectly so that the imbalance created in the economy by their past acts or misdeeds comes to an equilibrium.

1-15, December, 2014, Bureaucracy Today

♦♦♦

Government is nothing more than the combined force of society, or the united power of the multitude, for the peace, order, safety, good and happiness of the people.

— John Adams

14

Tackle Corruption by Positive Actions Forward

Corruption has become such a powerful demon that it cannot be destroyed easily. The best way is to keep it engaged in positive actions by an official organization so that it may not raise its head.

Corruption is manifested through bribery, fraud, stealing public resources, partiality/favouritism, the use of public assets for private purposes, etc.

The infection of corruption has spread at every level and in every section of society in India. From morning to evening, one comes across various forms of corruption. People of late have become very conscious and volatile as most of the money goes down the drain of corruption unlike in earlier days when only a small percentage used to be wasted in corruption. Secondly, it has become so widespread and powerful that things are not moving in the country.

It is, therefore, essential to ensure that things move fast in the Government as well as in the private sector so that people don't have time to organize themselves for corruption. Delay breeds corruption. If delay can be done away with, corruption cannot stand and will evaporate. Continuous economic growth and development will engage corrupt people in worthwhile engagements so that they do not have time to make a strategy for corruption and implement it. Speed will storm the bastion of corruption. Secondly, the disaster by slow economic growth will be avoided. Some State Governments like those of UP,

Uttarakhand, Madhya Pradesh, Delhi, Jharkhand, Himachal Pradesh, Kerala, Karnataka, Jammu & Kashmir, Odisha, Assam, Bihar and Punjab have come up with specific laws that any public servant who doesn't deliver the service on time, will be penalized. But such laws and regulations are not being implemented by superior officers either due to their involvement in the corrupt chain or due to the fear of non-cooperation from their subordinates. The Government of Punjab has set up a State-level commission called the Punjab Right to Service Commission which can even take *suo motu* notice of failure to deliver service and penalize even those superior officers for non delivery of service, or inaction by them. This has created confidence in the public which voted for the Akali Government in Punjab. In Bihar also, some action on these lines has been taken under the Bihar Right to Public Service Act, 2011 but the spirit is now tapering off. In Bihar, even assets created out of corrupt booty were acquired by the Government and are being used for public purposes like schools, etc., or are being auctioned in public and proceeds are deposited in the public exchequer.

In India, initiatives such as citizens' charters, the RTI Act, social audit, the redressal of public grievances and Lokayuktas have done a wonderful job. But now the corruption lobby even is trying to hide the citizens' charters, etc., from public view in government offices. The Lokpal and Lokayuktas Act, 2013, which has been enforced at the initiative of public activist Anna Hazare is a precious weapon in the hands of the people of India. Even the Prime Minister is within the ambit of this new Act. The Lokpal has power of directly conducting inquiry and launching prosecution and no prior approval of the Government will be required by the CBI in respect of cases entrusted by the Lokpal Act. However, Group C & D employees have been indirectly excluded from the purview of the Lokpal Act.

The public in general has interaction with Group C &D employees everyday and their main grievances are against these field level employees and inspectors. It is hoped that the States will take cognizance of corruption cases against Group C & D employees of the Central Government through their Lokayuktas. The State Lokayuktas should have concurrent power to inquire and report to the Central Lokpal or to the Central Vigilance

Commission. However, whatever has come down to the public to tackle corruption from the Government is appreciable. The Acts and Regulations to tackle corruption should also be accountable to the public through the concerned legislatures. Their review reports at least once in two years should be placed before the State Legislative Assemblies and Parliament respectively. Necessary amendments may also be carried out from time to time in anti-corruption laws, rules and regulations or executive instructions based on public feedback to make them more dynamic, organic and public welfare-oriented.

16, April, 2014, Bureaucracy Today

♦♦♦

> *Effective leadership is putting first things first. Effective management is discipline, carrying it out.*
>
> **— Stephen Covey**

15

Legal Approach to Combat Corruption

India is rated as one of the most corrupt countries in the world. Corruption is the major problem in India's advancement. The best measure to reduce corruption is through legal processes.

The *Indian Penal Code* as originally drafted by Macaulay, had contained effective provisions in Section 161 to tackle corruption by punishing the giver and taker of the bribe. In the long run, the bribe giver didn't come forward to lodge FIR or complaint with the police or magistrate and the criminal justice system became blind towards ever-growing corruption. As a result, the Britishers handed over good number of corrupt personnel along with the independence.

The *Prevention of Corruption Act. 1947* was bought in force just after the independence. It was declared as a cognizable offence. The acceptance of gratification was punishable and the burden of proof was shifted on the public servant to prove that he didn't accept or attempt to accept illegal gratification. However, the terms trivial gratification or habitual acceptance of gratification didn't allow the law to spread its wings. Secondly, the punishment was from one year up to seven years. But for special reasons, it could be less than one year.

However, the law provided that police officer not below the rank of Inspector could investigate the offence. This was also a stumbling block. Further permission of Superintendent of Police was required to investigate the crime. Over and above, previous sanction of the Central Government or State Government was required for prosecution. The statement of the bribe giver was not subject to prosecution under Section 165A of the IPC.

The 1947 Act, with its glaring deficiencies, failed to achieve its purpose and India gradually climbed up the ladder to become one of the top five corrupt countries in the World. This enfeebled developmental efforts of popular governments at the Centre and in the states. Thereafter, **the Prevention of Corruption Act, 1988** was brought into force. Then, the definition of public servant was extended to cover elected representatives and office bearers of government and semi-government bodies. A Special Judge for every area was appointed though he could not become fully functional. The punishment was increased from six months to five years. Even demand or solicitation by a public servant amounted to the commission of the offence. Exercising influence with public servant and abetment are also punishable. Even obtaining valuable things without payment is punishable. This Act, at present, is the main instrument to tackle corruption in India.

As per Section 22 of the Act, 1988, the proceedings sanctioned by it, cannot be adjourned but this provision is observed more in breach rather than in compliance by the Trial Courts. The politicians as heads of executive avoid giving permissions for prosecutions; rather they find it more beneficial to blackmail such officers and use them for their benefits or for the benefit of their party. However, the governments have to exercise proper discretion before granting permission for prosecution because in case of liberal permissions, the bureaucracy will stop taking decisions unless bureaucrats are also punished for indecision or delay in decision making, which is very much required.

Section 13 (1) (e) gives wide amplitude of power to the police and the judiciary to punish a public servant if he cannot give satisfactory account of property disproportionate to his known sources of income. The burden shifts to the accused person to prove his innocence once the criminal misconduct under Section 13(1).(e) is proved by the prosecution. The Supreme Court in its latest judgment has held that there is no need to obtain sanction for prosecution if the charge-sheet clearly establishes the offence against the public servant under Section 12 for abetment of offence. This is a landmark judgment of the Supreme Court in the case *CBI Versus Parmeshwaran Subramanian & Another* (2009) 9 *SCC* 729.

There is a **Commission's of Inquiry Act, 1952,** which also provides appointment of the High Powered Commission to make inquiry into any definite matter of public importance which definitely includes major incident of allegations of corruption in public life. After all, through corruption, it is public money which is drained out for illegal purposes. But these reports take lot of time for publication and these commissions have become pastures for retired officers and retired judges. By the time the report comes out, people are no longer interested in the issue and the reports are so complicated that another Commission will be required to implement the report.

The **Central Vigilance Commission** has been doing yeoman service to catch corruption by public servants and officials posted in banks and other public undertakings. Had it not existed, banks and Central PSUs would have been sold off by this time. It has Vigilance Officers under it in every ministries, banks and PSUs of the central government who directly report to the CVC. They have been effectively implementing the provisions of the Prevention of the Corruption Act, 1988.

The **Lokpal Bill, 1998** was another land mark in the area. Lokpal at the Centre is to inquire into any act or conduct of any person other than a public functionary after giving opportunity of hearing to the other side. The Lokayuktas in various States have created ripples in the sea of corruption but actual punishments have yet to be reported because all these important cases ultimately land directly or indirectly in the High Court or Supreme Court. Secondly, the Lokpal and Lokayuktas have powers to submit reports but actions, can only be taken at behest of the top political executives who generally don't approve of actions. Therefore, these reports are allowed to gather dust and become outdated. Thirdly, the exceptions of the highest offices in the states or the Union Governments stand out as eyesores in this legal process.

The Foreign Exchange Management Act (FEMA), 1999 was to regulate foreign exchange. In spite of FEMA, lot of money was repatriated to India, which was black money kept by the Indians abroad and was siphoned of from India in foreign banks.

To tackle all loopholes, the **Prevention of Money Laundering Act, 2002** came into force, which was further amended in the year 2009. The Act intends to confiscate amount involved in crime or which are intended for commission of crime, like terrorism etc. This will also control payment system like Havala in India for these crimes. It also provides for attachment of property including its confiscation. However, the Courts are to designate a Special Court out of one or more Courts of Sessions. This means additional pendency of cases in already overburdened courts.

There are adequate safeguards or legal provisions to combat corruption in India. However, the machinery to implement the same including police, CBI, quasi-judicial authorities, and the judiciary has to play their due role to save the nation from decline.

16–31 December, 2010, Business Economics

♦♦♦

16

High Time to Follow UN Convention on Corruption

The United Nations Convention 2005 prescribed a series of measures for preventing corruption, which include formulating and implementing effective anti-corruption policies and practices, constituting preventive anti-corruption bodies and adopting a transparent system for recruitment and promotion of civil servants. It also prescribed steps to institute a regulatory and supervisory regime for financial institutions in order to deter and detect money laundering.

Surprisingly the UN has reached the conclusion that even giving loans to the developing countries is more of a burden on their economies because the aid money is misappropriated by unscrupulous contractors in connivance with bureaucrats at all levels. As a result, UN agencies have withdrawn many aided projects all over the world.

In such a global scenario, bureaucrats have to decide all over the world whether they want to lead their professional life as per a code of conduct or to disturb their mental peace and equilibrium by indulging in corrupt practices and expose themselves and their ill-gotten assets to public gaze, criminal prosecution and seizure by the same Government of which they have been part and parcel. If the bureaucrats escape from departmental action by their erstwhile brethren in the bureaucracy and a dilatory judiciary, the media and public opinion will drag them into the dragnet of exposure. Their patrons, that is the top bureaucrats and top political executives, have become so unpopular with the public, because of their corrupt practices and inability to control the corruption of their subordinates, that they will not be able to provide them a protection umbrella or shelter. This is the greatest contribution of today's Information Technology exposure, especially the proactive social media like Facebook that the public in general has the last judgment to pass on any event of public interest and the persons-in-authority cannot overlook their exposure and comments.

As the bureaucrat is a public servant, his each and every action is related to public interest as he draws his salary or compensation from the State exchequer which is made of contributions from the public at large. Therefore, every bureaucrat is also directly accountable to every member of the public. Thus, a corrupt official will not be able to manage his misdeeds as there is an unending chain to be satisfied which will not be cost-effective for him. Bureaucratic corruption also comes clearly in public domain through the exercise of the Right to Information.

Even undemocratic rulers are likely to be sensitive to public opinion if they wish to avoid civil unrest. A free Press is a good check, especially in undemocratic countries that lack other means of constraining politicians and bureaucrats. Ultimately the media will fail if it focuses on lucid scandals to increase its ratings and may not have any real interest in reforms that can help reduce the flow of corruption stories for it to cover.

In that case conscious individuals and groups will push for a change. Thus, there seems to be no escape for corrupt bureaucrats from the dragnet of law and public censure. It is a different matter when a bureaucrat indulges in corruption suppressing his inner voice or psychology. In that case, he will have to stand on trial as an ordinary criminal. As far as society is concerned, bribe money or black money is mostly utilized as ostentatious expenditure and for unproductive purposes. It is even sometimes used to finance illegal crimes of terrorism, drug trade and human trafficking and even for changing democratically elected governments. Thus it is high time to follow the UN Convention on Corruption to fight out and finish corruption to a zero level.

1-15 August, 2016, Bureaucracy Today

◆◆◆

Government is a contrivance of human wisdom to provide for human wants. Men have a right that these wants should be provided for by this wisdom.

– Edmund Burke

17

Ombudsman in India

Lokayukta around the world is known as Ombudsman. It is an institution to prevent misuse of bureaucratic authority. It is a dynamic institution to ensure administrative justice which is gradually disappearing around thc World.

The institution of Ombudsman owes its origin from the Scandinavian countries which hardly have any traces of corruption. Lokayukta or Ombudsman was appointed in 1809 in Sweden. Denmark in 1962, Norway in 1962 and New Zealand in 1962. In the course of next three decades, the office multiplied rapidly, at the national regional and even municipal or grass root levels of government spreading throughout the liberal democracies of Western Europe, North America, the Caribbean and pacific region, and some parts of the Middle-East, Africa, Australia and most parts of India.

In democracies, the government changes by the people's change of mind. The new set of political executives come on the issues, like removing of corruption and providing transparent and expeditious government action. Therefore, bureaucrats can not prevent Ombudsman from being placed to oversee their corrupt practices. They have to mentally accept its existence and co-operate with the Lokayukta. Even a dictator can not prevent this institution to come into existence. He can only delay its establishment. Thus, the public officials and staff have to re-orient themselves and convince their families that every paise of extra income through corrupt means is vitiated with adverse consequences in his service records. He will have to be prepared to be prosecuted, forgo his promotion and to go to jails. This is a sour pill but it has to be accepted by the most powerful bureaucrat.

The awareness among citizens now-a-days is very high in view of all prevailing internet and active social media. If the government tries to suppress a thing, it will be exposed through media via social media in which every person has freedom to express.

THE INDIAN SCENARIO

India is very much behind the race of establishing this institution at the national level known as Lokpal inspite of promulgation the Lokpal and Lokayuktas Act, 2013 due to ego clashes rather than on the issue of some principle. So far, about 99 countries have made this institution active in their jurisdiction. Even countries are setting up Ombudsman at following six levels;

1 All purposes and all levels of government,

2 Specific purpose ombudsman like for minorities or Scheduled Castes and Scheduled Tribes,

3 At international level of governance,

4 Human Rights Ombudsman,

5 In-house complaints redressal mechanism,

6 Private Sector ombudsman like Banking Ombudsman, Media Ombudsman or Consumer Ombudsman.

However, India even does not have all purposes Lokayuktas in all States. The office of Lokayukta exists in Maharashtra: (1971), Bihar (1973), Rajasthan (1973), Uttar Pradesh (1975), Madhya Pradesh (1981), Andhra Pradesh (1983), Himachal Pradesh (1985), Karnataka (1985), Assam (1986) etc. It has been proved in India that the institution becomes effective according to the person-in-position. Lokayuktas of Madhya Pradesh, Karnataka, Maharashtra, Andhra Pradesh and U.P. have done commendable jobs. But the Ombudsmen in many states in India and countries remain under employed as there are not many cases or complaints of corruption before them. In Scandanavian countries, people have not heard of corruption by police on street or by a petty government staff to expedite a genuine work in their government office which is rampant in India and many Asian, African and Latin American countries. The corruption has become an indicator how much developed a country is.

The Lokpal under the Act, 2013 will be a multi member body. Its jurisdiction extends from the peon to the Secretary of the Department, Government of India and from the constable to the Prime Minister of India (after retirement). Even the NGOs, societies or trusts are included within the fold of the Act. However, to make the institution of Lokayukta and Lokpal successful at the Centre, Special Courts are to be set up simultaneously so as to complete trial of cases within the prescribed period of one year. One good feature of the Act is that the Special Court can assess the loss caused by the action or decision of the public servant in a conspiracy with the beneficiary. Such loss may be recovered from the both proportionately. Some States infamous for corruption have done a tremendous good job by retrieving their reputation in the field of corruption by attaching ill gotten properties mainly immovable properties and putting them for public use like opening schools in those properties. Other States will follow the suit soon as public in India is no longer prepared to tolerate corruption as their way of life at least in cases of public servants involving public revenue or public fund which they deal with as trustees of the public.

Thus, success of the institution lies in the society's response to the transparency and integrity. The institution is nevertheless worth an effective trial and not a lip service to it alone.

♦♦♦

18

The Dilemma of a Bureaucrat

After the historic judgment of the Supreme Court in the Coal Blocks case in 2014, there was a hunt by the Central Bureau of Investigation (CBI) to bring the officers involved in the scam to book as the apex court held the method of allotment from 1993 to 2011 invalid since allotments were made "without application of mind, without assessment of comparative merit and without following guidelines". HC Gupta was the Secretary of the Coal Ministry and many allotments were made during his tenure.

Gupta was one of the members of the prestigious Competition Commission of India when this bomb exploded. He resigned as his name surfaced in the case to face investigation and trial on moral grounds. Gupta is the topper of the 1971-batch of the Indian Administrative Service and an ideal for many bureaucrats for his simplicity, honesty and establishing milestones. Most bureaucrats know that he hardly owns any property in spite of serving the Government for more than 40 years in the IAS.

Every bureaucrat is pained to read that Gupta has been booked in many cases under the Prevention of Corruption Act, 1988 read with relevant IPC and CrPC sections. As Chairman of the Screening Committee having a dozen members, including, the Chief Secretary of the concerned State Government, Gupta got the allocation proposals approved by the then Prime Minister who was also the Minister of Coal at that time Gupta was shocked when he found that CBI Judge Bharat Parashar had handed him charges of conspiracy and corruption and misguiding the then Prime Minister. He has to be in the court for long hours and has to pay for lawyers beyond his means so much so that nothing will be left over for his only son and wife to survive. He writes in his petition before the trial Judge, "However, it is quite possible that at the end of the trial the court may find me guilty. This will not change truth as far as I am concerned. However, if that happens I would like to be punished with most severe penalty/punishment."

The CBI can well trace the trail of money allegedly paid in the scam and should accordingly choose officers out of all the powerful members of the Coal Blocks Screening Committee. If the CBI cannot prove *mens rea* in the case, it has no locus standi to drag a former IAS officer to trial for its "inefficiency" in investigation. Gupta's simple application to file his common defence statement in other cases and for a common trial involving the same offence to avoid repetition and personal harassment has been turned down by the trial court and the highest court of India. It means that after his retirement, he should spend the rest of his life defending his actions during service. Can't the Government give legal help in such exceptional cases?

The Supreme Court has passed judgments that there can be no discrimination between a Joint Secretary of the Government and other public servants and there is no requirement of seeking sanction to prosecute a government servant. No public servant is entitled to the protective umbrella of Section 197 of the CrPC. Although Section 197 of the CrPC refers to Judges also, hardly any prosecution of a Judge has been sought under this section.

One cannot rely totally on the investigation of the CBI which recommends many innocent persons as guilty. The CBI could not bring any accused person to court inspite of spending money three times on the foreign travels of its officers for investigation into the Bofors Gun case and the wanted rich persons like Vijay Mallya and Lalit Modi are still beyond the reach of the Government of India.

NON-POLICE EXPERTS

To keep pace with the fast decision-making process in this age of Information Technology, the CBI should have non-police experts and even IOs for inquiries into corporate governance and the ways of senior civil services. India cannot afford one more policy-making paralysis Any CBI investigation should not be allowed to linger on for more than six months like in other countries. At the same time if political executives do not give sanction to launch prosecution within three months as per the Supreme Court's decision in the Vineet Narain case, the CBI should be authorized to file an appeal against such non-decisions which are very inimical to the administrative system. Or if no sanction is received within three months, it should be "deemed sanction". Investigation agencies should also not behave like caged parrots humming the tunes of their political masters but follow the lawful orders of their superiors as per the decision in the Nuremberg Trial.

It is hoped that the honest Government officers like HC Gupta are not harassed after their retirement.

I think it is time the Government recognises its honest officers and protects them rather than prosecuting them.

IAS ASSOCIATION'S SUPPORT

Coming in support of Gupta, Sanjay Bhoosreddy, the head of the Central IAS Association, says, "An honest civil servant should not be harassed by anybody or agency or institution while in service or after- retirement. It would make the civil servants working in the system nervous and edgy, which would not be in the interest of the country."

Niti-Aayog' Chief Executive Officer Amitabh Kant has also voiced his support for the former Coal Secretary. "He (Gupta) is the most honest officer I have come across in my entire career. The chargesheet against him is real travesty of justice. It is a sad and tragic moment," Kant, a retired 1980-batch IAS officer of the Kerala Cadre, tweets.

Civil servants also feel that the CBI which has filed chargesheets against Gupta lack officials who can understand the nuances of functioning of officers of the Secretary level. "Although the CBI nowadays is increasingly investigating cases of myriad nature right from those of corporate finance, international taxation, company law and banking, its manpower continues to be much less multi-disciplinary than one would expect," a senior serving bureaucrat tells.

His observations, find' tandem with Bhoosreddy's views.- "Error in judgment has to be looked at differently. We urge all the authorities that if a civil servant is found corrupt, then please deal with the matter harshly and jail him till his life. However, there is a need to protect honest civil servants from any kind of harassment for taking decisions in good faith and in public interest. It is pertinent to emphasise that an error in judgment should not be treated as criminal misconduct as it would highly demoralise civil servants," he says.

And it is no rocket science to understand that a demoralised and demotivated bureaucracy is highly detrimental to the task of taking India on the path of progress and prosperity.

1–15 September, 2016, Bureaucracy Today

♦♦♦

19

Civil Service Reforms: Need of the Hour

Various commissions and committees have recommended far-reaching reforms to make civil service personnel fully accountable to the community they serve. Taking their cognizance, the Supreme Court directed to constitute independent Civil Service Boards at the Centre and State levels. Many Governments have yet to implement this order of the Supreme Court..

Earlier the Hota Committee in 2004 recommended inter alia: (*a*) To provide toll free telephones for the service redressal system, (*b*) To designate one officer who should receive phone calls from members of the public and address the issues raised by them and resolve public grievances, (c) Employees and officers should wear name badges with job descriptions in brief, (*d*) Amendments to Article 309 and Article 311 of the Constitution of India to constitute Civil Service Boards and combat corruption, (*e*) Annual evaluation of the performance of a government department by an NGO or by a third agency or person, and (*f*) A fairly senior officer should be designated so that he may be able to reply to some of the queries of the caller or applicant and can also explain the cause of unreasonable delay in the matter of the caller or applicant or procure information from the officer concerned and send his reply fast.

There was a good system to display phone or mobile numbers of officers outside every office but this system has gone into disuse slowly because of transfers of officers and lethargy in updating the phone or mobile nos. For such a lapse, the head of department must be held responsible.

As regards reforms in the police system, the Justice-Malimath Committee (2001) stressed the constitution of a State Security Commission whose recommendations should be mandatory for the selection of Director General of Police. The DG will be selected by a panel of three senior-most police officers. There should be a Police Establishment Board under the DG for transfers and postings up to the level of DSP. This will tone up police investigation and reduce corruption in the police.

There should be fixed minimum tenures for the Chief Secretary, the Director General of Police and senior Secretaries of the Government of India. In case a premature transfer is needed, the officer should have the right to approach a three- member Civil Service Ombudsman set up for the purpose. In such a situation, the bureaucrat will work with peace of mind and will deliver his best to the Government and society.

The second Administrative Reforms Commission in 2008 and the Hota Committee earlier recommended for the enactment of a Civil Services law which will cover all personnel holding civil posts under the Union Government. In fact, such a law should be like the administrative law at present prevailing in informal shape in India and statutory law in France and other countries. This will be like a code of conduct for all civil servants as well as for the Government. It should be made enforceable. Otherwise in India, it will lose its edge.

To enforce the RTI Act, 2005, it is essential that all orders of senior officers or political executives should be in writing so that the information sought for by a member or member of the public can be provided without delay.

Political executives have nothing to fear if the Indian bureaucracy becomes more independent and impartial. The bureaucracy will become more efficient. For the public in general, better service delivery at the lower levels is required which can be achieved by introducing reforms like the system of wearing name badges and having designated officers to attend telephone calls as suggested by various Civil Service Reforms Commissions and Committees.

16–30, September, 2015, Bureaucracy Today

◆◆◆

> *The executive of the modern state is but a committee for managing the common affairs of the whole bourgeoisie.*
>
> **– Karl Marx**

20

SCPC Mandates Govt Servants to Perform

The Chairman of the Seventh Central Pay Commission in his foreword to the report says that if India wants a dedicated bureaucracy, then it will have to provide a good leadership and good governance. This aim will be achieved when an atmosphere of trust prevails and when Government employees are absolutely sure that their "trust shall not be betrayed and they shall be treated with dignified fairness". Then only the concept of good governance can be concretized. *(SC in 2013 (2) SCC516).*

On the other hand, the public is seriously concerned with the delivery of services by the bureaucracy which has not improved after the expectation of earlier Pay Commissions. Adequate funds are not left over with the Government for social welfare schemes after meeting the pay and perks of its employees. In compliance with the recommendation of the Sixth Pay Commission something was done but results were not observed on the ground. Only the biometric system to ensure the punctuality and attendance of officials has been implemented in selected offices.

Korea, Chile, Malaysia and the Philippines have implemented the Performance Related Pay (PRP) principle for their civil services and have considerable experience in using this as a tool for boosting performance and accountability. In Brazil and Indonesia, the PRP has contributed to reducing staff absenteeism.

The Seventh Central Pay Commission has provided guidelines for the Performance Related Pay which must be simple, transparent and easy to implement. It should be effective in rewarding good performance and managing poor performance in a targeted manner. It should be consistent across departments with enough autonomy to design context-specific criteria, targets and indicators. It should be non-additive at the end of the financial year as one – time incentive. Proper training and capacity building should go side by side.

This also requires making the Annual Performance Appraisal Report more objective and should be based on Results Framework Documents (RFD) which are an important anchor for determining Performance Related Pay. The Commission lays down more weight on work than personal attributes (60:40). The Commission is in line with the foregoing norms recommended to link the bonus scheme with increased profitability and productivity under well-defined financial parameters.

DICHOTOMY

As present, an individual officer can be rated excellent while the rating of the department could be lower. This dichotomy is to be removed. As a result, there will be huge peer pressure to perform which an employee will find it difficult to overlook. In the present system, the archaical boss-subordinate relationship is not effective. It should be replaced by a monitoring system by peers or beneficiaries.

The Pay Commission has suggested assessment indicators or Key Performance Indicators (KPIs) such as "timelines" which include presenting timelines for drafting, reviewing and taking decisions. These should invariably be reflected in Annual Performance Appraisal Reports to have real effect on the performance of a government servant.

All is not lost. After the implementation of the Sixth Central Pay Commission report, the Results Framework Document system has taken firm root in the Indian bureaucracy now and has emerged as a powerful tool for the evaluation of actual achievements of a department against annual targets. After the delay of 10 years, one can hope that the Performance Related Pay system will be introduced without any further delay. This will create more public faith in the bureaucracy and will ensure that India joins the ranks of developed nations and becomes the third largest economy of the world.

16–31, December 2015, Bureaucracy Today

◆◆◆

In a country where the sole employer is the state, opposition means death by slow starvation. The old principle: who does not work, shall not eat, has been replaced by a new one who does not obey shall not eat.

— Leon Trotsky

21

Before Motivating Others, Motivate Yourself

This is a great formula not only in management but also in routine life. Gandhiji always practised what he advocated. Motivation in work is a great challenge for the modern management. The government management has become so much pro-employees, especially in developing countries like India, that it has adversely affected other areas, including industries and service.

We must identify motivational levers which management is not only in a position to operate, but whose effects produce a favourable-long-term balance of advantages over drawbacks. Success in today's business or manufacturing organizations requires a much broader vision, not only of the organization itself, but also of people who make up the organization, their skills, competencies and competitiveness, their relationship to the organization which may be termed their work culture.

We must also understand why one employee works at less than 50 percent of the standard and another works at over 150 percent of the standard. The motivational tools are macro-environment or societal work climate, financial incentives, personnel management, job enrichment and leadership.

An employee doesn't work in vacuum. He is a part of society. He looks at the work culture around him and is influenced by that. Secondly, proper environment at a workplace and a rotational change of job should be provided so that employees may enjoy their work. Financial incentives play the most important role in the USA but in Japan and India, factors like permanent employment are equally important.

As regards personnel management India-born Nobel Laureate Amartya Sen in his book *"Equity Redefined"* places more emphasis on recruitment than other factors like promotion, appraisal and transfer. According to Prof. Sen, an objective and just system of recruitment or placement can do wonders. It can change the whole work environment and ethos. However, a few others place more emphasis on training. But it is an experienced fact that employees or workers keep on bothering more about their transfer, promotion and in-house appraisal than any other factors. And the idea of motivation is to motivate the existing work force rather than to recruit or procure an already motivated work force.

Leadership plays an important role in motivating subordinates or followers. The top leader should be nowadays technically well versed. Once Jamsedji Tata was travelling in an aeroplane. His seat broke down. He immediately took out a screwdriver and repaired the chair. Everybody around was surprised that the owner of such a big industry house could repair his chair himself. He said how he could ask his workers to use machine efficiently unless he himself knew something about it practically. Similarly, when R.C. Bhargava, Chairman of Maruti India, asked one of his operators to operate the lift properly, he retorted saying that it was not a simple job as running an office. Bhargava, IAS (retd), came back and operated the lift. That demonstrated his personal skill to every worker around and it infused lot of motivation among workers, operators and officers of Maruti Suzuki.

Gradually, familial loyalty or personality cult is losing an edge. Lack of motivational climate is one of the main reasons for ills affecting our industrial and governmental output. If this continues, there will be production even below the break even level, the quality of production will also be low and our rupee against the dollar will keep on slipping. The Indian Army presents a nice example of leadership. In a conflict, the casualties of officers in the Indian Army are more than in the case of any other Army of the world.

Nowadays, the workers have become very conscious. They would not obey a leader who preaches something but practises a different thing. Therefore, personal example has become the most important factor in present-day motivation in the field of management.

It is high time that the manager or administrator in a private or government organization should lead by self-example to motivate his team.

November 2013, Bureaucracy Today

◆◆◆

> *Let us sacrifice our today so that our children can have a better tomorrow.*
>
> **– A.P.J. Abdul Kalam**

22

Only Administrative Law is the Solution

The longstanding solution to all problems of the Indian bureaucracy is to bring about a codified administrative law in India. The piecemeal treatment will not be effective as the disease is quite acute. The Law Commission in its 14th Report has also recommended the same. Administrative law and administrative courts are working successfully in France.

One good result of the proposed law would be that an independent body will review every administrative action. Secondly, administrative law, if enacted, will also be a code of working for government officers and staff. Functionaries of semi or local self-government bodies will also be covered under this law. Thus the need to have various kinds of legislation to tackle different ills of the bureaucracy will be fulfilled. All rules and regulations can be broadly codified under this law. Thirdly, it will be easier to apply such a code or Act at the lowest level of the bureaucracy.

Consumers are very much fed up with delay and corruption in the functioning of government machinery. The administrative system is becoming gradually indecisive and inactive. Senior officers are always afraid of a review of their actions or decisions by High Courts or the Supreme Court.

How can this problem be solved and a healthy balance struck so that administrative actions or decisions may become not only just and fair but also speedy? The lack of speed is the only reason why India is still in the comity of developing nations. Senior civil officers are left alone to face courts when there are contempt of court cases against them. Actually subordinate officers down the line have no sense of proportion or judicial bent of mind to put up their notes, suggestions or drafts before senior officers so that they may speedily take just and fair decisions.

Solutions are manifold. Some of them will suggest that there should be proper recruitment methods. The second school of thought will suggest extensive training, retraining and continuous training up to the clerk level in the bureaucracy for human resource development. This is not feasible at present because training itself will involve a huge government expenditure and development of large infrastructures. The simplest solution is to have an administrative law in India. This law, if enacted, will lay down powers and duties of administrative authorities with emphasis on official functioning. It will cover all officials right from the peon to the Cabinet Secretary or from the constable to the Director General of Police.

The Indian administrative law in the codified form may consist of the following topics:

(*i*) The concept of natural justice as propounded by the Supreme Court of India and accepted by the general body politic of the country.

(*ii*) General guidelines for government officers and other members of the staff while arriving at a decision or making a suggestion on a file or in a note.

(*iii*) The accountability of bureaucrats for delaying their decisions or causing omissions in decision-making which should be equally punishable under administrative law. A member of the bureaucracy should also be personally liable to the Government if the latter suffers a pecuniary loss due to his latches or malafide decisions. He should be asked to make good the financial loss to the Government in terms of penalty or a fine. There should also be appellate fora to reconsider such pecuniary fine and penalty which will consist of bureaucrats only. This will be like a regulatory authority having specialized persons as its members. This will eliminate the element of arbitrariness or subjectivity against government employees. This function can be performed by Administrative Tribunals already constituted in India.

This whole body of law, rules and guidelines will help members of the bureaucracy to enlighten themselves regarding their rights, duties and decision-making process in the bureaucratic organization which is intricately linked with the progress of society or the nation. Thus, the chances of their bonafide errors in decision-making will be less. Many cases will not go to courts delaying the matter further for decisions. Last but not the least, the public will be greatly benefitted by a just and fair decision-making process at various levels and will put its faith and trust in the bureaucracy.

April 2013, Bureaucracy Today

◆◆◆

23

How American Bureaucrats Function

The bureaucracy or bureaucrats in America have historically contributed to the efficiency and effectiveness of the entire process of governance keeping pace with the time. The bureaucrats have thus integrated their values to support and develop responsible governance for the liberty loving Americans. The bureaucracy has become a condition of freedom, especially in view of the recent upsurge of corporate scandals in the United States.

Virtually every aspect of daily life is regulated to some degree by one or the other of the numerous administrative agencies that make up the national bureaucracy of America. The powers of these agencies are extensive, being judicial and legislative in nature as well as executive.

The US President is a very powerful Head of State. Therefore, he controls the bureaucracy rather the bureaucracy controls him as in many other small countries. Some of the instances below make the concept clear.

THE NEW DEAL

Roosevelt was a very assertive American President. He didn't like various branches taking decisions even like ship building without his approval. The President only came to know through the *New York Times.* Roosevelt's New Deal policy was to have committed bureaucrats around. However, gradually the policy got diluted and converted into a merit system and career bureaucrats like in India became more active in their positions because their mandate was to take the economic system ahead. But conflicts among administrative agencies like during World War II known as "battle of Washington" also surface here and there.

ENRON'S FAILURE

Company executives were not too concerned about America's laws. Enron decided to have its vision, and its new ad campaign, around a concept called "what we believe". Those beliefs included the wisdom of open market and "being a laboratory for innovation". This was a corporate equivalent to moralist libertarianism. They circumvented-energy market regulations and accounting laws. This annoyed the State bureaucracy and the Enron's top managers were jailed for offences committed and the corporation went into liquidation. It was established that Enron officials had bribed Indian politicians to set up a naphtha plant for power generation in Maharashtra and had manipulated accounts to deceive the audit. Resultantly the company's auditors PWC were also held guilty by the bureaucracy to manipulate accounts of Enron Incorporation.

WATERGATE SCANDAL

Watergate was a major political scandal that occurred in the US in the 1970s and the Nixon Administration attempted a cover-up of its involvement. It included bugging up the offices of political opponents in the Watergate building in Washington DC and other suspicious people. As a result of proved misuse of powers, President Nixon resigned on August 9, 1974. The scandal also resulted in the indictment of 69 people. Fortyeight of them were found guilty, including top Nixon Administration officials.

President Nixon first refused to hand over the recorded tapes. On the order, he handed over the tapes which proved his involvement. Facing near-certain impeachment in the House of Representatives, he resigned which is the only incident so far in American history.

BILL CLINTON, Former American President

MONICA LEWINSKY

FAILURE OF CIA IN IRAQ

The Central Intelligence Agency (CIA) misguided the American Administration that Iraq had weapons of mass destruction and there was an imminent threat. However, no such evidence was found after the US and the UK succeeded in a change of regime in Iraq after removing Sadaam Hussein. Later the CIA was instructed that it should improve its analytical processes to avoid this kind of error in the future.

CLINTON-MONICA LEWINSKY AFFAIR

President Bill Clinton was having intimate relations with one of his interns, Monica Lewinsky, at the White House. His flirtation with the young lady made a laughing stock in the US. However, on inquiry, the sex scandal couldn't be proved against Clinton and it was more or less a consensual amorous play. Had it been proved as sex exploitation of his employee, the most powerful public servant of the US had to resign. In moralistic countries like India, it is sufficient for a highly placed person to at least resign. Thus, America believes in equality at a workplace for men and women.

SUCCESS STORY OF EMERGENCY ADMINISTRATION

Minutes after the first plane hit the World Trade Centre in Manhattan on the morning of September 11, 2001, the Director of Emergency Management for New York City activated an Emergency Operation Centre on the 23rd floor of the WTC. There, without consulting the Mayor, he closed all streets below the canal, as well as all tunnels and bridges around Manhattan. Suddenly his centre's offices were hit by flying debris, so the Director moved the Emergency Command Centre to a WTC lobby. From there he arranged for the Coast Guard to seal New York's harbours and the Defence Department to block its city's airspace. The Transportation Commissioner rerouted buses and ferries to remove people from Manhattan. The Director and the master of the commuter train to New Jersey, standing on the concourse beneath the WTC, ordered an incoming loading train to skip the WTC stop and return to New Jersey. In the opening hours of this tragic day upwards of 3, 000 people were safely removed from the scene of this historic disaster.

CONCLUSION

The public likes to see American bureaucrats working more efficiently than the private sector. At the same time, they will

continue to be paid lower compensation than their counterparts in the private sector. Bureaucrats can be held liable and accountable as regards various schemes of their departments and can be asked to pay fines for intentional delays and indecisions. Thus there is growing realization among Americans that public servants or bureaucrats must be more efficient, honest and sincere so that the mission of the welfare of the last man in society is achieved by bureaucrats.

16–28 February, 2015, Bureaucracy Today

♦♦♦

> *No one is above the law and no one is below it; nor do we ask any man's permission when we ask him to obey it. Obedience to the Law is demanded as a right, not asked as a favour.*
>
> **— Theodore Roosevelt**

24

Role of Police in India's Development

The traditional role of the Police Department is to control crime in society and help the Government realize revenue so as to run the administration. Nowadays, the third important job of development is also being entrusted to the already overburdened police. Policemen are not always available to assist in development work saying that they are busy in apprehending criminals. But the rate of crime in India is on the increase.

Earlier the police set-up was fully under the control of the District Magistrate. The DM used to solve many law and order problems in the bud or after a flare-up by providing development doses. Similarly, paramilitary forces are doing a wonderful job of providing assistance to citizens in Naxal or terrorist-affected areas. Now the Police Department has been demanding lot of autonomy and much of this has been provided to it. But that has not resulted in a better law and order situation or peace in Indian society.

The Police Department, it is said, doesn't bother to give protection to development works undertaken by the Government, panchayats or contractors. In the past, policemen used to be instrumental in realizing Government revenue. Now they shirk the responsibility of helping realize revenue which is also used to maintain the police organization. They take the alibi that the revenue dispute being a civil matter is outside the purview of the Police. At the same time people have observed that police authorities happily surrender to be used by politicians for their vested interests. Thus, one finds that the Police fends for itself. As a consequence, the Police loses public support which is its real strength. At present, people generally view the policeman as an exploiter or a moneytaker.

SOCIAL CHANGE AGENTS

However, everything is not lost on the police front. The newly recruited members of the IPS, who are young and tech savvy idealists, are trying to play the role of social change agents so as to make India a fast-growing economic power. The computer is extensively being used now in many services by the police administration, including getting passport hurdles cleared, managing international border checkpoints and even the filing of FIRs. Social observers say that Indians are very much wary of not getting their FIRs being registered at the concerned police stations inspite of all claims and declarations in this regard. The District Superintendents of Police, the Director General of Police and the Commissioner of Police in metro cities claim to entertain FIRs online. But hardly action is taken on those FIRs unless one goes to the police station physically and does the formality. This is a very sad experience in India which none would like to face. The general impression is that businessmen and industrialists avoid interaction with the police and keep their investment low.

Those who are in the know of things say that at present, Government officials do not like to register even their departmental cases with policemen as they are mostly non-cooperative and non-responsive. Similarly, grassroots level semi-government institutions like panchayats, municipal bodies or engineering departments are averse to approaching the police as policemen allegedly consider them involved in unholy connivance with their contractors which is not always the fact.

What is the solution? Yes, the solution lies in giving a professional touch to the police. There should be public accountability and public audit, a performance appraisal based on objective considerations and transfers and postings by an outside independent agency. In foreign countries, HR management of police organizations is being carried out by outside professional agencies. According to Nobel Laureate Amartya Sen, there will be 33 per cent improvement in efficiency in a government organization if the recruitment is fully transparent and objective. It is equally applicable to the police organization.

1-15, September, 2016, Bureaucracy Today

♦♦♦

They have come to think that they are born to be trodden under the fear of the wealthy. They have to be given back their individuality........Service of a poor is the service of the God.

– Swami Vivekanand

25

Bureaucratization of India

Recent trends indicate that India is moving towards bureaucratization as a nation. The bureaucracy is an instrument to achieve the goals of development and upliftment of the masses. The bureaucracy as an organization works through formal rules and procedure. Rules become superior to results. Bureaucrats take decisions on a day-to-day basis which impact the life of people. Therefore, people are interested how the bureaucratic system functions. But it is very difficult to know its real working. It is opaque and lives in its own cell or limited group. Political superiors or dictators are the supreme bosses of bureaucrats.

In a developing country like India political executives are gradually being cut off from the masses except in panchayat bodies up to the block level where they are directly accountable to people. Political executives find it very easy to work as a part of the bureaucratic set-up because they have not to answer anything promptly as there is the joint responsibility factor. Thus, they can relax in a cozy environment of office and work without any accountability.

Everybody in India tends to become a bureaucrat. Even this infection is catching fast in private organizations. It is very surprising that many retired bureaucrats have written memoirs which bring out the internal working of hitherto known as secret services like the Intelligence Bureau (IB), the Central Bureau of Investigation (CBI) and even the armed forces.

Earlier, the public did not pay heed to the decision-making process in a bureaucratic organization and used to say - "This is your business. We are only concerned with results."

During the Nehruvian era, politicians while going in for elections used to blame the bureaucracy and the public also used to believe them. But after Mrs. Indira Gandhi, the slain Prime Minister, misused the bureaucracy as her own committed body, politicians dare not go back and tell at the hustings that they could not fulfil their promises because of an inept and inefficient bureaucracy. They have become part and parcel of the system and want to enjoy its fruits more than bureaucrats. Therefore, when a political executive is blamed even for changing an affidavit for his political or his party's political gain, he is indefensible. At present Ministers like to control day-to-day government decisions rather than taking policy decisions or launching public-oriented schemes or goals. Ministers are more interested in transfers and postings of officers which ensure their hegemony in the office or department. Therefore, the public knows well that it is the Minister or political executive who is responsible for all the good work or mess in the public service. The media only focuses the violation of procedure in special cases and some of the freelancers rush to the court under the garb of public interest litigation that due to a violation of a rule or procedure, the rule of law has been violated. And the court sits on the same and the public debate goes on and on. Out of the above, members of the public get nothing except some juicy stories which they can neither understand nor are they relevant to their life-setting. Bureaucrats are happy that their procedure and not the output is in the public domain.

In India, the basic needs of the teeming millions are yet to be met. Secondly, there are natural calamities like drought, etc. Such stories should find prominence in India. The bureaucratization of India is a dangerous trend. The mission of public welfare should be kept in focus. The bureaucratization only generates delay and corruption which will further frustrate the people whose continuous motivation and enthusiasm can take India ahead.

1–15 April, 2016, Bureaucracy Today

♦♦♦

26

Computer is the Biggest Bureaucrat in India

The answer has come out from inside the computer. We cannot change. You have to approach the computer headquarters where the main server, *i.e.* the top boss, is located. The Government or the power centre has fed this output that has been given to you. None can change unless the policy fed in the computer is changed. Even the Prime Minister, the Chief Minister, the Minister or the Chairman or the Managing Director cannot do anything to help you.

The maxim to use the computer is - "Garbage in, Garbage out. " The computer is a machine and it has its own limitations. The men behind the machine are equally important. They have been entrusted with certain discretion and power to solve the problem. Had it not been so, the computer would have been placed without any assistant. If the man behind the machine refuses to exercise discretionary power, the machine cannot be blamed. The machine is as much heartless and indifferent as a bureaucrat if not more. A bureaucrat is one who is formal, rule or procedure-bound and does not bend rules even under pressure. Thus the computer is also a bureaucrat as per the Weberian model of the bureaucrat.

SOFTWARE OWNER LOSES CONTROL

Instructions are fed in the computer through a well-thought software prepared after thorough discussions in the department with experts and users in that area or problem and issued for use by the department or the organization after its quality test at various levels and after removing defects pointed out or the inclusion of various left out problems or facets and their solutions. Once it is released in the public domain, the owner of the software loses its control and it operates like a tiger in the jungle. Human genius knows no bound. One cannot provide solution to all foreseeable contingencies. As a result, it fumbles or roars in its area without any external control. To hide their failure or lack of proper exercise in its making, the department or organization keeps on shifting responsibility on its users or beneficiaries or consumers or customers or clients.

In the garb of security of personal data or privacy, the software has been made specially by banks that even the computer expert customer finds it difficult to open his own account. Only officials of the organization owning the programme can handle it. This causes injustice to its beneficiary. But there is none to correct the fallacies or replace it by another software which is time consuming and cost effective. During this period, the computer with its particular software acts like a super boss.

It is a fact that the top man in the organization does not devote that much time in the making of the required software or programme nor does he like to provide lot of discretion in unforeseen contingencies fearing its misuse by the machine as it was done in the past by the person-in-position who was given discretion by Parliament or the Legislature under Acts or statutes or by the Government in its rules, regulations or procedures. It is a common experience that discretion had been more exercised based on subjective or partial considerations rather than based on objective considerations and on the principle of justice and equity.

UNBRIDLED POWER

Today the computer has been left in the public domain with unbridled power and discretion. For example, if a bank deducts credited amounts or debits against hypothetical charges without prior intimation to the customer to maintain the minimum balance in the account, the bank employee sitting before the computer expresses helplessness and undertakes no corrective measure. If the customer goes and complains to the Public Grievance Mechanism, its official first ask the complainant to file a complaint in his name through his or her own E-mail.

In India, there is not so much computer literacy developed that everybody has his own E-mail nor a general person has a computer or advanced mobile to handle e-mails. As a result, the hapless customer or client or a member of the public keeps on suffering and prays when a favourable decision will come out from the black box of the newly created god in India or the world. The persons handling the main server are apt in handling the giant machine and they pay hardly any heed to a new type of public grievance or the public. The departmental officer sitting with the giant machine is either inactive or is not given due importance or scope or time to handle an unforeseen problem before him.

In an ideal situation, discretion to the person behind the machine should not be obliterated all together but proper supervision and control should be in place to see that it is exercised with due care and just consideration. Machines like computers are there to help the man but not to overpower him completely which is happening now-a-days in unhindered application of computers in all fields without any back office control.

1–30 November, 2017, Bureaucracy Today

♦♦♦

27

Yoga: The Therapy for Bureaucrats

In a democracy, the public is the master of bureaucrats. Thus they are under constant surveillance. This causes much tension and stress to bureaucrats and they develop a lot of occupational diseases. Their job creates most of the diseases in them. If they remain healthy and happy, they can contribute better for the well-being of society.

Bureaucrats should be provided with such a therapy that they may not fall ill and continue to work their best for the progress of the country. Yoga is the only therapy which caters to positive healing and healthy living.

This ancient Indian physical and mental therapy has now been recognised by the United Nations by declaring June 21 as International Day of Yoga. The UN Secretary General, Ban Ki-Moon, has appealed to all the citizens of the world to follow Yoga. The Secretary General is the first bureaucrat of this world. Let all bureaucrats around the globe follow in his footsteps.

Yoga maintains a balance between the body and the mind and the mind and the spirit. If bureaucrats can maintain the balance between the body and the mind, they will give a better output at their workplace. For this purpose, Yoga has been introduced in most of the training centres of bureaucrats when they enter the Service and even do mid-career courses. Such Yoga consists of a few *asanas* and *pranayama*. The *asanas* lay emphasis on physical postures whereas *pranayama* as a breathing exercise takes out lot of negativities from within the system and fills the body and the mind with fresh air and positive thinking. Yoga also helps in regenerating body cells which make a man healthy. However, when Yoga is used to cure a particular disease, it is to reduce the hyperactivity tendency, especially in the case of the psychosomatic disorders induced by abnormal stress and strain. In India, there is no dearth of Yoga coaches.

In India, Baba Ramdev appears almost everyday on television to demonstrate how to practise Yoga. Shri Shri Ravi Shankar, Founder of the Art of Living' organisation, has a proven therapy, *'Sudarshan Kriya'*, to make the body and the mind healthy.

I am sure that the bureaucrats who have missed Yoga training at the Academy or at any other training centre, will now adopt this practice and make themselves healthy and happy to contribute more to society, which is their duty. For bureaucrats, ultimately Yoga lies in uniting with their duties and performing them efficiently.

1–15 October, 2015, Bureaucracy Today

♦♦♦

> *Yoga is the philosophy of the life and action capable of ensuring individual and collective welfare. It makes one work without discrimination and with equality achieving samatva (justice).*
>
> **— Swami Ranganathananda of R.K. Mission**

JUDICIARY

28

Judicial Reforms: The Need of the Hour

Judicial reforms have become a great challenge to the polity because there is undue delay in the disposal of cases in India. Justice delayed is justice denied.

It is, therefore, essential to provide a speedy and efficient judicial system. At present, there are about 30 million cases pending in various Indian courts. Out of these cases, about 26.8 million were pending in the District Courts and 4.5 million in the High Courts as on December 31, 2013. About 66,000 cases were pending in the Supreme Court as on July 1, 2014. Other special courts like Consumer Courts and tribunals may account for a total pendency of about 15 million or more cases. The cases in the High Courts and the District Courts are pending for about five years on an average. The Supreme Court has shown the way by reducing its pendency from about 1,04,936 cases as on December 31, 1991 to 22,551 cases as on February 22, 2002. The process is still continuing. The steep decrease in the pendency of cases in the Supreme Court is due to concerted steps taken by it, viz the fixing of cases and their allocation to Benches through a computer network, the grouping and classification of cases involving similar questions of law, the setting up of specialised Benches and the computerisation of records.

Fifteen factors can be said to constitute total judicial reforms. They are as follows: Judge strength and appointment of Judges; Procedural laws, Quality of substantive law; Court procedure;

Court's mechanism/demeanour, including intentional delays by parties; Working hours of courts; Service of court notices and submission of reports including investigation reports, etc. to courts; Delay in the delivery of judgments; Training of Judges; Quality of legislative drafting; Observance of professional conduct by Judges; Quality of the Legal profession and legal education; Alternative disputes resolution and the setting up of tribunals - conciliation and arbitration as part of regular proceedings; Setting up of *Gram Nyayalayas* and infrastructural facilities for the judiciary.

In criminal cases, granting adjournments should strictly be avoided. If Judges or Magistrates still give adjournments, the cost of the same should be reclaimed from them, and paid to the affected parties as suggested by former Law Minister Kapil Sibal.

Advocates should co-operate with the courts and applications intended to delay the proceedings should be avoided.

To tackle the long pending sessions cases, more Fast Track Courts should be set up. These Fast Track Courts are disposing of sessions cases and important criminal cases involving undertrials on a priority basis. They have been proved effective in controlling the crime situation in States like Rajasthan, Uttar Pradesh, Bihar and Maharashtra. Gram Nyayalayas when set up and operated would be wholly informal and not technical. These courts will help in reducing the pendency of trivial matters at the grassroots level. The Law Commission in its 154th Report has suggested that other States should adopt the pattern of the Andhra Pradesh Mandala Nyaya Panchayats Bill, 1995.

The computerisation of courts is a very popular scheme in the judiciary and the Union Government has been allocating funds under the Centrally Sponsored Scheme every year.

Facilitation/Enquiry Centres have been set up in the Supreme Court and almost in all High Courts where the litigant people can know the status of their cases on the Internet and on voice mail. Computerisation has reached almost all the District Courts in the country but it is yet to be fully made operational.

The judiciary is a responsible part of the State. I am sure that the judiciary will itself implement necessary reforms.

16–30, September, 2014, Bureaucracy Today

♦♦♦

Law harasses the poor and wealthy rule over the law.

—Oliver Gold Smith

29

Delay Denies Justice

Society exists because justice is there. Law is not an end in itself but is an instrument to secure justice. Justice sometimes is also termed *dharma.* Salmond defines law as the body of principles recognized and applied by the State in the administration of justice. Thus the rules, notifications, regulations, etc, made and implemented by the executive branch of the State form part of law and should aim at delivery of justice. Delay in decision-making by the executive branch has caused havoc in denying rights of people and hence denied them justice.

Any administrative action which violates the principles of equality can be scrutinized by courts based on the mode of exercise of power. As per the basic concept of law, omission is as much punishable as commission. In the garb of omission, indecision or inaction the bureaucratic system is getting scot-free for delay which is causing huge losses to society and the State For example, delay in decision-making in the Sardar Sarovar Dam Project has caused a revised cost of project on the higher side by a few thousand crores of rupees. This is frequently heard that government or semi-government projects have been delayed because of the avoidable delays in decision-making causing losses worth hundreds of crores of rupees each year. This is a common experience that after the budget is passed, the release of money itself takes four to five months to sanction. Thereafter, hardly optimum time is left for proper implementation. It can be managed easily by shelf of schemes. It is said that there is a cut even in the release of funds. The public is suffering for not getting licences, passports or birth certificates on time. It is a fact that overwork causes corruption. Members of the public think that government officials often indulge in gossip on their seats or do some idle work rather than attending to their grievances. There is not much use of approaching either the departmental public grievance unit or the departmental vigilance cell. Therefore, there is unanimity that delay is the most dangerous enemy of India. It induces or causes corruption. If India has to tackle corruption, its source i.e. delay should be curbed in the bud.

Some members of the public are of the opinion that even ministers or panchayat or municipal representatives should be punished for delays.The delay in decision-making whether intentional or unintentional should be equally punishable.

At the same time, the end fruits of delays *i.e.* amassing of wealth by public servants should be ploughed back to the public. If we crack delay, the base of corruption will automatically fall down. This major source of corruption has to be tackled first. On various protests from the public, the Government of the NCT of Delhi has brought the Delhi (Right of Citizen to Time-Bound Delivery of Services) Act, 2011 into operation but its implementation is yet to take off. Like the RTI Act, non-reply or inaction under the Act should be made punishable to activate the sleeping giants of the bureaucracy. Similarly the Government of India through the Department of Administrative Reforms and Public Grievances has placed "the Right of Citizens for Time-Bound Delivery of Goods and Services and Redressal of their Grievances Bill 2011" before Parliament. It is hoped that this Bill will be passed soon. This along with the Lokpal Bill will be good assets for the public. The public should learn how to use these weapons in its hands more intelligently, cleverly and fearlessly through NGOs, enlightened citizens and elderly persons in the locality.

The Delhi Act, 2011 provides that Rs. 10 will be charged for each delay from a government servant causing delay in the matter. It is also provided that in case a government servant causes more than 25 defaults in a year, he or she will be given a show-cause notice. However, it should be replaced by departmental proceedings and departmental punishment. It should also be ensured that the supervisor or controlling officer should also be held liable for delay by his subordinates. It should be recorded in his Annual Confidential Report. It is also to be ensured that senior officers on their own inspect various files of subordinate public servants and punish them even without applications from affected members of the public. Only then this Act can be made really useful for the public. Otherwise it will move very slowly. In the case of the Central Bill, it is good that citizens' charters are being given statutory recognition.

July, 2013, Bureaucracy Today

♦♦♦

The acid test of any legal system is not the greatness or the grandeur of its ideal concepts, but whether, in fact it is able to produce order and justice.

— Lee Kuan Yew,
First Prime Minister of Singapore

30

Adjournments as Curse to the Judiciary

The Indian judiciary suffers from lot of delay in the disposal of cases which results in mounting arrears in courts. One of the reasons for the delay is frequent adjournments sought by lawyers and which are granted by courts liberally. There was a revolutionary amendment in the year 2002 in the Civil Procedure Code, providing in Order 17 Rule 1 that no adjournment shall be granted more than three times to a party during the hearing of a suit, but the experience till date shows that this part of the statute is observed more in violation than in observance. It is surprising that this provision which was brought as the ground norm in the civil procedure law in India is unknown to most of the judicial and legal fraternity. Even if it is referred to in courts, it is bypassed as an unimportant feature, but everybody knows that it was included in spite of a strike by lawyers all over the country.

The judicial system consists of judges and lawyers and no judicial system can achieve its purpose unless both cooperate. One of the main causes of delay in the disposal of cases is frequent adjournments. It starts from the day cases are filed. Plaints or suits are not filed with all required papers and the rigmarole continues with the filing of more papers. Even with replies or written statements, all requisite papers are not filed. Thus it seems that delay is inbuilt in the very psyche of the Indian people.

Moreover, lawyers take adjournments on various grounds *inter alia* the illness of the lawyer or the party to the suit, the advocate's engagements in other courts, the non-receipt of all the papers and documents from the client, a fresh appointment of an advocate by the client, a prayer for the transfer of a case from one court to another and last but not the least, the absence of a presiding officer from the court, either due to he or she being on leave or busy otherwise.

In spite of clear statutory provisions that adjournments will not be granted on flimsy grounds taken by lawyers and heavy costs are to be imposed, the position is otherwise. It so happens that when the case is right near the decision, the advocate who feels that the decision will go against his side immediately moves for an adjournment on some alibi or another by filing some interim prayer which palpably is new but which is part of the whole case.

If courts become strict about reducing the arrears and disposing of cases swiftly, all the problems can be solved, but it is observed that courts also work at ease to deliver their judgments, for which the time-limit prescribed is 60 days. As a result, the public is losing faith in the justice delivery system. Whenever they go to the court with the hope of getting an order, they mostly come out with the next date of hearing and even pay fees to the advocate as the matter is usually adjourned.

Interestingly, there are also some clients and advocates whose vested interest is only in delaying the judicial process, especially in matters of huge arrears of taxes, fees and other arrears, and dues to the Government. It can be scientifically observed that when the case file is to be brought to the court, it takes about one hour in taking out the file from the record room, listing it by the assistant concerned and placing it in the court by the court attendant. Thus, the precious time of the court is wasted while granting adjournments. One minute working of the Delhi High Court entailed an average expenditure of ₹ 14, 771 in 2011-12. With such a great amount of taxpayer's money going into working of the courts, the system gains nothing from adjournments.

The legal fraternity overlooks the fact that majority of the clients and bonafide litigants come before courts and tribunals with the hope that their petitions/cases/applications will be expeditiously disposed of and will not end up filling up the dockets of courts for years and the lawyer's pocket. Even generations have to wait for orders from the source of justice in the country. Judgments/orders are implemented not because there is enforcement machinery but due to the faith of the people in the judiciary. It is, therefore, hoped that all will work unitedly so that the curse of adjournments on the Indian judiciary is wiped out.

1-15, July, 2014, Burcaucracy Today

♦♦♦

The law of Triviality briefly means that the time spent on any item of the agenda will be in inverse proportion to the sum involved.

– C.N. Parkinson

31

Accountability in Higher Judiciary

The Indian judiciary can no longer remain in a close circuit. It has already expanded its wings to public domain through its pro-activism on social, economic and administrative issues via the Public Interest Litigation (PIL) system. The public has-been attracted towards the judiciary and looks forward for the protection of its interests by it.

Two Bills, namely, the National Judicial Appointments Commission Bill, 2014 and the Judicial Standards and Accountability Bill, 2012 deal with the appointments of Supreme Court and High Court Judges, and the accountability and transfers of Judges of the High Courts and the Supreme Court.

The 2014 Bill has already been passed as a constitutional amendment by both Houses of Parliament and is awaiting approval by more than half of the State Legislatures before becoming an Act. Therefore, the PIL filed in the Supreme Court to set aside the Bill was graciously dismissed by the Hon'ble Supreme Court in the first phase though allowed later on and declared it as unconstitutional assailing one of the basic features of the Constitution i.e. independence of Judiciary.

Both the Bills are supported mainly on the ground that the Higher Courts cannot be judges in their own case or causes. The Bills are being opposed because they might undermine the independence of the judiciary which is one of the basic features of the Indian Constitution as per the law laid down by the Supreme Court in the Kesavananda Bharati case of 1973.

The opponents of the 2014 Bill argue that the National Judicial Appointments Commission consisting of the Chief Justice of India, two seniormost Judges of the Supreme Court, the Law Minister of India and two eminent persons will be controlled by the Executive. But this is not a fact to be afraid of because any two members of the Commission can withhold any recommendation of the Commission. The Commission has three judges of the Supreme Court and therefore, they have a veto power with them.

However, the main criticism against the present Collegium System devised by the Supreme Court in the S.P. Gupta case (1993) is that the Chief Justice of India has the final say in spite of reservations by the President who appoints Judges of the High Courts and the Supreme Court. It inter alia holds that the seniormost Judge of the Supreme Court should be appointed as Chief Justice of India. Thus, there is no transparency in appointments to the higher judiciary and adequate representation of women, Scheduled Castes, Scheduled Tribes, and members of the minority communities cannot be ensured.

Despite the academic criticism, critics of the present system of appointments could not find fault with the quality of Judges appointed except in a few cases of corruption and favouritism which is a likelihood in any given system today. However, the process of appointments took a long time and the High Courts always suffered from the lack of strength of Judges. As a result, the pendency of cases in the High Court has considerably increased and this is very detrimental to India advancing in the 21st century. However, in the new system, it will take even longer time because seeking the opinion of State Governments, the calling of meetings and getting the concurrence of views of all the members will be a herculean task to be shouldered by the not adequately equipped Department of Justice, and the slow-paced and less responsive. State Governments. Over and above, some quarters even ventilate that the opinion of the concerned Bar Council of a State should be sought before considering the nomination of a practicing Advocate. Thus, in a way, the Bill conforms to the basic working of the Constitution of India which is based on the system of checks and balances among the three organs of the State *i.e.* the Judiciary, the Legislature and the Executive.

The Accountability Bill, 2012, which lapsed before the 2014 Lok Sabha poll had certain clauses relating to the declaration of assets and liabilities of Judges on websites; procedure for filing and disposal of complaints against Judges, reference to the Scrutiny Panel and its powers; the functions and powers of the National Oversight Committee and the power of search, seizure, etc. to the Investigation Committee.

MECHANISM FOR INVESTIGATION

The Bill proposed to establish a credible and expedient mechanism for investigation into individual complaints of misbehaviour or incapacity of a Judge of the Supreme Court or a High Court. The stated misbehaviour includes wilful or persistent failure to perform the duties of a Judge, corruption or an act which amounts to moral turpitude of a Judge.

However, ultimately, the advice of the Oversight Committee presided over by a former CJI will be placed before Parliament which will be then introduced before the Joint Committee of Parliament. It is a fact that it cuts into some delay which got into files for impeachment of Judges of High Courts or the Supreme Court but it is not much different from the existing procedure which is not transparent at present. Also, the name of the Oversight Committee is confusing and ought to be changed to the Supervision or Overseeing or Review Committee. It will be better if India adopts a system of "Judicial Ombudsman" which will be synonymous with the "Parliamentary Ombudsman" as is prevalent in many countries so that there is a drastic cut in the long chain of decision making through investigation and scrutiny.

It is surprising that the Accountability contained norms of conduct by Judges like debarring them to fight any election even to a club or an association, and debarring their spouses, sons, daughters, sons-in-law or daughters-in-law and so on to use their residences for legal practice or even to give interviews to the media. If the Judges are expected to deliver judgments on PIL cases or on socioeconomic issues, they should not be kept aloof from society. There is no surety that a person in isolation will be a man of integrity whereas the reverse is more true on practical grounds. However, there is a provision of imprisonment of a person making a frivolous or a vexatious complaint, and this keeps a check on such nuisances.

This was high time the Judges Protection Act, 1985, for the subordinate judiciary and other judges of the tribunals or fora was also reviewed and revised simultaneously The public at large is more concerned with the enforcement of better standards and higher accountability by Magistrates and Judges of the lower judiciary, tribunals or fora. Thus, it is hoped that the new NDA Government in office will consider these suggestions while bringing the fresh Judicial Standards and Accountability Bill before Parliament for consideration.

1–15, October, 2014, Bureaucracy Today

♦♦♦

32

The Supreme Court has Shown the Way

The steep decrease in the pendency of cases in the Supreme Court is due to its concerted steps taken viz. the fixing of cases and their allocation to Benches through its computer network, the grouping and classification of cases involving the similar question of law, the setting up of specialized Benches and the computerization of records.

STRENGTH OF JUDGES

According to the Chief Justice of India, Justice T.S. Thakur, the Judge strength is the single most solution to tackle delay in the disposal of cases. He made an emotional plea and wondered during the Chief Ministers and Chief Justices' Conference in the presence of Prime Minister Narendra Modi in April, 2016, "Why it is not being done at the rate of 50 Judges per million population which has been recommended by various commissions and even by the Department-related Parliamentary Standing Committee on Home Affairs in its 86th Report." It has also been laid down by the Supreme Court in the *All India Judges Association* case that the Judge strength in India should be achieved at the rate of 50 Judges per million population in the next five years. The Central and State Governments accept this in principle without any concrete steps because it will involve a huge expenditure of more than ₹ 14000 crore, followed by a huge recurring expenditure. Secondly, Public Service Commissions and High Courts will not be able to recruit so many Judges.

Simultaneously Public Works Departments will not be able to construct additional courts and an increased number of residences in a time-bound manner. There are already huge unfilled vacancies of Judges in the District Courts to the tune of 2,200 judicial officers and there are vacancies of more than 150 Judges in various High Courts in the country.

The Supreme Court has struck down the National Judicial Appointments Commission Act, 2014 as regards the process of selection and appointment of Judges to the High Courts and the apex court and the accountability of Judges as threatening the independence of the judiciary as well as the separation of powers which are the basic features of the Constitution of India. Thus, there are differences on the Collegium system between the Supreme Court and the Union Government and the finalisation of a "Memorandum of Procedure" is still in limbo. If the Judge strength is increased in the next five years, it will help tackle the present pendency of cases and the subsequent pendency of cases which will definitely multiply in future.

CPC AMENDMENTS

The amendments in the Civil Procedure Code (CPC) in 1999 and 2002 may be termed a *magna carta* for the Indian judicial system. The amendments *inter alia* provide for time-limits at various stages of a suit like the service of a plaint to the defendant within 30 days of the institution of the suit even through courier, the filing of a written statement within 30 days extendable up to 90 days, examinations of witnesses through a commissioner as per the general power of court to extend the time up to 30 days, the delivery of a judgment within 60 days, compulsory pre-litigation settlement efforts and the restriction of a number of adjournments to three to a party.

ADJOURNMENT MAIN CAUSE OF DELAY

In spite of a clear provision in Order XVII, Rule-1 of the CPC, adjournments are taken on various grounds *inter alia* the illness of a lawyer or the party to the suit, the advocate's engagement in other courts, the non-receipt of required papers and documents from the client, the fresh appointment of an advocate by the client and a prayer for transfer of the case from one court to another. Sometime an adjournment is granted because of the absence of the presiding officer from the court either due to he or she being on leave or busy otherwise. As a result, members of the public are losing faith in the justice delivery system. Whenever they go to the court with the hope of getting an order, they mostly come out with the next date of hearing after paying fees to the advocate.

Thus, the precious time of the court is wasted while granting adjournments. One minute's working of the Delhi High Court entailed an average expenditure of ₹ 14, 771 in 2011-2012. With such a great amount of taxpayers' money going into the working of courts, the system gains nothing from adjournments.

The Supreme Court has held that the grant of an adjournment by a court has to be on showing special and extraordinary circumstances. It cannot be in routine.

WORKING HOURS OF COURTS

The courts in India are working for less days than government offices. The Shetty Commission has suggested that the vacation of District/ Subordinate Courts should be cut by 15 days and the District Court should work for at least 36 hours in a week. Litigants visiting the courts find that after the lunch the courts are not active. If the working hours of courts are increased by half an hour, lot of pendency of cases will be tackled.

ALTERNATIVE DISPUTE RESOLUTION

Section 89 of the Civil Procedure Code provides for a compulsory prelitigative settlement. The dispute before the court will be referred for settlement by way of mediation, conciliation or arbitration through a Lok Adalat or through a court-appointed mediator. According to the Supreme Court, 90 percent of the cases are settled out of court in certain countries where the Alternative Dispute Resolution (ADR) system has been successful. At the same time, free legal aid will be available with the proper implementation of the Legal Services Authorities Act, 1987.

Computerisation has helped a lot. Now daily court orders are available on the Internet and the website. Time is not far off when everything will be computerized and the courts in India will be E-Courts. However, it is still doubtful whether a litigant from a village will be able to take advantage of it immediately. However, to a large extent, litigants have been relieved of exploitation by their counsel as regards the fixing of cases and orders on various dates. Litigants can also get copies of a judgment from the Internet. In the Supreme Court and all High Courts, facilitation/Enquiry Centres have been set up where members of the public can know the status of cases on the Internet and on voice mail. There should be more financial autonomy to the courts so that they don't have to look up to the government for every small thing.

SETTING UP OF GRAM NYAYALAYAS

Gram Nyayalayas when set up and operated will be informal and not strictly technical. The expenditure of poor litigants will be reduced to a minimum and it would take justice at the doorstep of litigants.

In so many judgments, the Supreme Court has reinvented the speedy disposal of cases as one of the Fundamental Rights under Article 21 of the Constitution of India. The apex court has coined the term "judicial impact assessment" as is practised in the United States. It is hoped that the courts will invoke their inherent powers to make available justice to the public at their doorstep.

1-15, December, 2016, Bureaucracy Today

♦♦♦

33

Judiciary Needs More Judges

During the Chief Ministers and Chief Justices Conference held in New Delhi in April the Chief Justice of India, Justice TS Thakur, made out a well-meaning and an emotional plea to increase the strength of Judges in the country. The arrears of cases in courts are mounting day by day and have increased to an astronomical figure of over three crore in the District Courts, the High Courts and the Supreme Court. The main solution suggested is to increase the number of Judges in all courts.

The 120th Report of the Law Commission has laid down that India should adopt the US principle of Judge strength. In India, there are about 14 Judges per million population whereas in America, there are more than 50 Judges per million population. It means that India requires to add 40,000 Additional Judges in the District Courts.

There are more than 2,200 vacancies of Judges in the District Courts of India. The reasons are many. First, State Public Service Commissions do not recruit a large number of Munshiffs or Judicial Magistrates as it will adversely affect their other commitments to fill up vacancies. Secondly, experts from the judiciary do not find suitable candidates during interviews. As a result, even notified vacancies are not filled in. Even if Judge strength is sanctioned at 50 Judges per million, it will take more than 10 years to fill up the posts. Alternatively, the High Courts can hold special recruitment tests to fill up posts of Additional District Judges from among Advocates but this method also fails because of the dearth of suitable candidates. And many such recruitments are stayed or delayed by the same High Court on judicial side due to litigation on the grounds of corruption or procedural lapses.

It was high time the State Governments sanctioned new posts of Munshiffs every year and ensured that State Public Service Commissions hold special examinations to recruit judicial officers.

The posting of retired District Judges for further two years is a solution but the fear is that they may adopt the same dilatory procedure which they adopted during their tenure and brought the judiciary to this state of affairs.

Apart from posting retired Judicial officers, the following solutions can be tried with immediate effect:

- Existing vacancies should be filled up on top priority.
- More than three adjournments should not be given to a party in a case as per Order XVII, Rule 1 of the Code of Civil Procedure.
- The vacation period of District and Subordinate Courts should be cut by 15 days and the District Courts should work at least 36 hours in a week as against 48 hours working in other government establishments as per a recommendation of the Shetty Commission.
- Judgments and orders should be brief and concise and delivered within 60 days as per the CPC.
- Nyaya Panchayats should be set up alongwith Panchayati Raj institutions at the block level.
- A survey should be conducted to find out why the Fast Track Courts are not delivering results on expected lines.
- There should be closer and more stringent supervision of District and Subordinate Courts by their respective High Courts.

The above measures will not only provide a proper strategy to tackle the problem of huge case arrears but will also generate more faith of people in the judiciary.

16–30 June, 2016, Bureaucracy Today

♦♦♦

34

Huge Pendency of Cases in District and Subordinate Courts

The District and Subordinate Courts of India are overburdened with judicial cases and personnel to dispose them of are fewer as compared to the number of cases filed each day in the lower courts. This has resulted in imbalance and growing discontent among the masses following which they resort to extra-legal methods. The apathy of the lower courts lessens the faith of the commoner in the entire judicial system and needs to be addressed immediately.

The pendency of cases in the lower courts is a matter of grave concern in India. The figures published officially show that there were 2.74 crore cases pending in the District and Subordinate Courts as on March 31, 2014. The disposal of cases with respect to their opening balance was about 16%. There is always an increase in the pendency of cases by about 2% with respect to the opening balance. It proves that the case pendency will never be liquidated in spite of the best efforts by the judiciary and the Government, including the setting up of fast courts in India.

EFFECT ON THE PUBLIC

One of the causes of unrest and violence in Indian society is that legal disputes among persons are not settled by courts in time. Litigants go to courts with the expectation of early decisions or results but they come back frustrated with the adjournment of cases to new dates. Nani Palkhiwala, the famous jurist, observed that adjournment led to enormous misery for litigants and forced them to look for extra-legal alternatives. The Supreme Court on October 13, 2015 observed that the huge pendency of over 3.72 lakh cases in consumer courts, including 2.73 lakh cases in District Consumer Forums, shows that "nothing is working in these courts". In some States some members of the Forums hearing cases cannot even write two lines of an order in English.

SUGGESTED REFORMS

To tackle the pendency of cases, judicial reforms are essential to make the judiciary efficient and speedy. Providing more Judges and meeting the infrastructural needs of the judiciary are the two major steps. Other such steps are ensuring the service of court notices through the e-mail method and courier service as provided in the Civil Procedure Code (CPC). Summons can now be served by the plaintiff through registered post, speed post or through a courier along with its service by the court. This is a revolutionary change which strives to involve the plaintiff in the

service of summons and introduces a new system of serving summons through the courier which was earlier dependent on the age-old methods of service of summons (*Section 9 & 9A of the CPC*)

Section 89 of the CPC provides that before the commencement of proceedings in a case, the court will try to settle the case among the parties through amicable methods i.e. arbitration, conciliation and mediation and through the *Lok Adalat*.

Adjournment is the greatest curse of the lower judiciary. Order XVII, Rule 1 provides that no adjournment shall be granted more than three times to a party during the hearing of the suit. If this single provision is implemented with all sincerity by courts, the major cause of delay in the disposal of cases can be avoided. In this, the grand profession of Advocates has to cooperate with the courts in civil and criminal cases. Adjournments are taken on the grounds of non-attendance of witnesses and non-submission of investigation reports.

For this, police administration has to be geared up. Investigation and prosecution machinery should be exclusive. According to a recent amendment in the CPC, the judgment should be delivered within 60 days after the conclusion of case hearing. This will go a long way in early delivery of judgments in civil, criminal and other court cases in India. Ex Chief Justice of India, Justice HL Dattu has said,

"We have taken a decision that we will try our best to see that there is no case pending beyond five years. Five years will be the maximum for the old case."

SOLUTION

The setting up of alternative tribunals and courts is one of the solutions. At the block level, a *Nyaya Panchayat* should be set up. The *Gram Nyayalaya* will be wholly informal and nontechnical. If its expenditure is reduced to the minimum, it will make justice available from their own persons at the doorstep of litigants.

To implement these suggestions, the respective High Court has to play a vital role as the District and Subordinate Courts are under its supervisory control. There should be more accountability of the lower judiciary. However, to achieve full success the Government, the judiciary, the legal profession and the public have to co-operate.

16–30, November, 2015, Bureaucracy Today

◆◆◆

Justice is commodity which is in a more or less adulterated condition the state sells to the citizen as a reward for his allegiance, taxes and personal service.

— Ambrose Bierce

35

Consumer Grievance Redressal through Mediation

Consumer forums in India were established to provide simple and speedy dispute redressal. The quasi-judicial machinery at the district, State and national levels has been empowered to give relief and award compensation to consumers.

In view of the need for quick disposal of grievances, mediation has been incorporated statutes of various countries as a first process to settle disputes between the buyer and the seller of goods or the supplier of services by service agencies like transport, airline or tourist agencies.

In Germany, there are mediation NGOs at all important market places to give advice to consumers and settle their disputes amicably. In Spain, mediators have law degrees. Even lawyers are provided to consumers to file and pursue their cases free of cost by the Government. In Belgium, there is an ombudsman who tries to reconcile the parties before forwarding their cases with his reports to quasi-judicial forums for the disposal of disputes. To spread general awareness, consumer-centric magazines are published which have membership in millions in European Union countries.

In India, there are some best practices in vogue. There are helplines for consumers at the National, State and District levels. Consumer helplines note down problems or complaints of consumers, forward them to the agency concerned and provide a feedback to complainants. Well-known companies in retail fields have their public grievance officers who promptly attend to these complaints. Some States like West Bengal and N.C.T. Delhi have posted mediation officers at District Forums or a group of forums to first try to settle disputes amicably by calling both the parties. If it is not settled, the consumer is assisted in drafting his/ her complaint which is then filed in the concerned forum. At the district level, the Consumer Affairs Department is having a helpline. Its officials on receipt of a complaint at once contact the defaulting party and try to settle the complaint amicably. The major part of satisfaction is being received by Indian consumers in India through such informal channels.

MED-ARB PROVISION

There is a provision for mediation and arbitration *(Med-Arb)* to be availed of together for dispute resolution wherein a dispute referred to for arbitration can be mediated and the settlement termed a consent award. Justice Dalveer Bhandari, Judge, International Court of Justice, also advocates for the hybrid concept of *Med-Arb.*

As per Section 89 of the Code of Civil Procedure, every court in India, including consumer forums, should first try to settle the dispute before it through arbitration, conciliation, through Lok Adalat or mediation. Through Lok Adalats, a large number of commercial disputes are being settled giving relief to consumers. However, the scope of mediation is required to be enlarged considerably in India. As soon as it is done, the better it will be. Consumers are sitting on a volcano of discontent which may erupt any time in India resulting in a colossal loss of public property in violence.

The suggested ways are; allow District Consumer Forums to have mediation authority i.e., mediation should be permitted at the District forum complex or the Consumer Affairs Department in districts. Independent mediation centres can be set up in big cities like the capitals of States and metropolitan cities.

However, India is not yet ready to authorize NGOs for mediation due to the fear of unfair practices by them. In due course, mediation may be done by NGOs in India just like in Germany. However, free legal aid is available to litigants in India, including consumers. But one doesn't know how easily free legal aid can be actually availed of by consumers or customers. In the meantime, consumer education and awareness programmes for consumers may be run in a big way starting from the school level. The grievances of consumers may be settled through interactive sessions on the radio and television.

16–31, March, 2016, Bureaucracy Today

◆◆◆

Unnecessary laws are not good laws, but traps for money.

– Thomas Hobbes

36

Free Legal Aid : For Speedy Disposal of Cases of Jail Inmates :

An Experiment in West Bengal to the Law

Lok Adalats have been set up as effective mechanism for alternative resolution of disputes through persuasive and conciliatory efforts with the free legal aid to the poor under the Legal Services Authorities Act, 1987. The Lok Adalats have now been provided a statutory base and are vested with powers of civil courts. They are being extended to all the States and Union Territories. So far, the Lok Adalats have disposed of about one and half (1.5) crore cases. The Act has now been extended to create permanent Lok Adalats in selected public utilities where the order of the Lok Adalat will be final upto a claim of ₹ 10 lakhs. The Act of 1987 is also a benevolent instrument to provide legal aid to the poor and needy people. In fact justice has no meaning to the poor strata of people in India unless it is made inexpensive because they cannot afford to go to the regular courts. There are 30 per cent people below the poverty line in the country and their condition is that they find it difficult to make both ends meet in their life. Therefore, they cannot be expected to pursue their court cases if they are implicated in some civil or criminal cases and therefore, the court becomes an instrument of exploitation unless they are given financial assistance to fight cases. The legal aid system naturally defends or strengthens their cause.

The Supreme Court has also held, (in ME Rao Hosket Vs. State of Maharashtra (AIR) 1978 SC 1548), that it is the duty of the State to provide legal aid to the poor. The Lok Adalat along with legal aid to the poor can work as useful arm of the present day judicial institutions. Along with this alternative method, it is of utmost importance that endeavour is made that the litigants find it is cheaper to compromise than to take their dispute to any court for resolution of their controversies.

Section 89 has been added by the Civil Procedure Code (Amendment) Act, 1999, which provides for compulsory pre-litigative settlement. The dispute before the court will be referred for conciliation or settlement by way of mediation, conciliation or arbitration through Lok Adalat. This also refers to the 129th Report of the Law Commission of India. It is, therefore, considered necessary to set up permanent Lok Adalats every day in each district in the country so that the parties can approach these courts for settlement of their disputes before they are stuck up in courts. For most of the dates in courts, hearing is limited to extension of dates, adjournments of case or injunction granted. The litigants keep on seeing towards the court for final decision like a farmer who looks towards the sky for rains during the month of June. It is expected that the popular governments will place adequate mechanism for providing relief through the fora like Lok Adalat where people can go and settle their disputes before regular proceeding starts.

As per the request of the Chief Justice of India, Chief Judicial Magistrate or Chief Metropolitan Magistrate are holding courts in jails once or twice in a month to hear cases of undertrial prisoners who are languishing in jail for a long time without any trial and are unable to pursue their cases due to poverty or other reasons. The suggestion made by Hon'ble Chief Justice of India to Chief Justices of High Courts had some salutary effect. He has also appealed to hear the cases of senior citizens of the age of 65 years and above on priority basis by various courts in the country and to dispose of cases which are more than 7 years old on priority. Such initiatives had positive effects and have substantially contributed towards judicial reforms.

Free Legal Aid to the Inmates of Prisons in West Bengal

The State of West Bengal has implemented the West Bengal Correctional Act, 1992 for the first time in the country. It takes care of correction and reformation of prisoners as well as amenities to them. As one of the important measures, it was tried through aegis of West Bengal Legal Services Authorities to provide free legal aid to various prisoners in 53 correctional homes in the State. It was instructed that legal aid lawyer will be earmarked for each correctional home at the level of Central Correctional Home, District Correctional Home and Sub-divisional Correctional Home and Special Correctional Home.It was done with a view so that jail authorities cannot take the plea that they could not contact the earmarked advocate for the legal services to the prisoners.

Secondly, the earmarked advocate could also visit the correctional home freely and collect the cases and data from each correctional home. Then the cases or the petitions of the prisoners could be dealt by him personally in the law courts or through some other legal aid lawyer. This was primarily meant for the Undertrial prisoners (UTPs) who were sometimes languishing in jails for a long time. Even their rights have been well reiterated by the Supreme Court for early hearing in Common Cause Vs Union of India, R. D. Upadhyay Vs State of Andhra Pradesh and other cases. In R. D Upadhyay Vs State of Andhra Pradesh, the Supreme Court observed, "keeping in Jails such a large number of prisoners is of no justification. It was suggested that the State will be well advised to see that the Police should be directed by the State concerned to file the challans within a reasonable time and to see that the Magistrates concerned hold trials in the jail premises itself. By this way not only the trials can be effectively conducted but also those who have already undergone a substantial sentence and also who may not be required to be kept in the jails, can be released. Such is one of the effective steps that has to be taken by the States."

The status of this experiment in various correctional homes in West Bengal is as follows .

Alipore Central Correctional Home

It has about 2,000 inmates. Legal aid lawyers have been earmarked and they are visiting Alipore Central Correctional Home on each Thursday. Cases are handed over to them and they also talk to the prisoners concerned. Critical cases are handed over to them but the progress of final disposal of cases is not known. The disposal is not at the required pace. So far, nine (9) prisoners have been released through assistance of District Legal Services Authority from April, 2004 to February, 2005.

Presidency Correctional Home

This is also a very important correctional home at Kolkata. This houses about 2,000 prisoners. This correctional home has a good impact of the new system. One Sri Ranjit Chakraborty, Advocate of the District Legal Services Authority has been earmarked. He puts up all such cases before the District Judge, Alipore Court. During last three months, he has taken 171 petitions from various prisoners out of which 5 have been released and three advocates on behalf of legal aid authorities have been conducting their cases. 23 case histories are being dealt with by them as full cases. Petitions are by UT prisoners confessing guilt, praying for advocate at government cost, praying release on PR Bonds, praying release on bail and early disposal of cases etc. However, there is no action in respect of the cases of the prisoners who are related to nearby Howrah and Sealdah courts. It is seen that legal services authorities of district Howrah and Sealdah have to be activised so that they can also fail in line with the District Legal Services Authority of Alipore District Court. On the other side, the system of submission of petitions by the Welfare Officer has been equally working efficiently. The Welfare Officer filed 316 petitions independently out of which 91 prisoners have been released and three have been convicted.

Dum Dum Central Correctional Home

Four advocates have been earmarked by the District Legal Services Authorities, 24-Parganas (N). But nobody has turned up so far. Jail authorities are taking up the cases with the District Judge and Chairman, District Legal Services Authority and the Chief Judicial Magistrate but it seems that these advocates are not interested because they have more lucrative cases elsewhere.

Midnapore Central Correctional Home

The District Legal Services Authority have nominated four advocates. They regularly come to the correctional home. They give free legal consultation to the prison inmates specially UTPs. They do appear on their behalf in the court. However, there is a gap between consultation and representation. Petitions were submitted by the Welfare Officer on behalf of prisoners. Positive results are forthcoming.

Berhampore Central Correctional Home

Nothing has been done. No initiative has been taken by the jail authorities nor by the District Legal Services Authority.

Jalpaiguri Central Correctional Home

There is a happy outcome of the new system introduced in the Jalpaiguri Central Correctional Home having about 1000 inmates. Legal aid lawyers are visiting the Correctional Home. They are appearing on behalf of the prisoners. Shri Manoj Dutta Chowdhury who is the nodal lawyer, is monitoring the cases on behalf of the District Legal Services Authority. So far 21 cases have been taken up by them and five prisoners have been released on bail. But some of the prisoners are not able to set free because they are not able to pay bail amounts.

Burdwan District Correctional Home

One gentleman advocate and one lady advocate are regularly visiting jail w.e.f. December, 2004. With their intervention, 14 numbers of UTPs have since been released on bail and 8 number of UTs though granted bail, not yet been released for want of bail amount.

Siliguri Special Correctional Home

Sub-Divisional Legal Services Authority, Siliguri has taken some initiative to work out modality for free legal aid system but this system has not been put into action so far.

CONCLUSION

From the perusal above, it is clear that proper steps have been taken by the State Level Services Authority and also by the Deptt. of Jails. But the progress varies from correctional home to correctional home. The progress is not satisfactory at the sub-divisional level which should be done by the state level intervention. However, in cases of Central Correctional Home and District Correctional Home, the following suggestions can be considered for implementation,

(*a*) Where there is a nodal advocate with whom the jail authorities can contact, the progress has been better than other places where group of lawyers have been earmarked. Therefore, one advocate should be earmarked with each correctional home in the State.

(*b*) Where there is active cooperation from the jail authorities, the progress has been better. Thus, the jail authorities have to play role as equal partner in the matter

(*c*) The advocates from the Legal Services Authorities are not appearing regularly perhaps because either they are not well paid or they are not at all paid.

(*d*) Something should be done to arrange for the bail amounts for the poor UTPs who are not able to pay their requisite bail amounts.

(*e*) District Monitoring Committee consisting of District Judge, District Magistrate & Superintendent of Police should be activated so they can help in quick disposal of cases of undertrial prisoners.

♦♦♦

37

Role of Mediation in Settling Consumer Disputes

A case study of West Bengal

People are afraid of going before the Courts whatsoever simple procedure or inexpensive procedure may be like the procedure before the District Fora, State Commission or the National Commission. There is a hiatus between the Judge and the petitioner. Secondly, in spite of liberty to appear himself, the petitioner appears only through the Advocate. He is not able to say his prayer directly before the Forum or Commission. Therefore, there is always a gap and the consumer as the petitioner is not satisfied. Advocates and judges love procedure. Mediation can overcome this difference.

It is now well established that there is no problem in adopting mediation as a tool to solve consumer disputes, though mediation has not been mentioned specifically in the Consumer Protection Act, 1986. The word used in the Act is settlement of disputes and not the suit or case. Section 89 of Code of Civil Procedure provides that every Presiding Officer of the Court should try to settle the dispute between the parties by way of reconciliation, mediation or arbitration before the regular case is taken up for hearing by the Presiding Officer. According to Section 13 (2) (a) of the Consumer Protection Act, 1986, District Consumer Dispute Redressal Forum will try to settle each dispute. That is why Advocates are not mandatory to appear before Forum or Commission.

To make the provision of Section 89 of CPC successful, it is essential that there is one officer present in every Court who can work as Mediator and settle the disputes between the parties amicably. The Forum and Commission are overburdened with cases, disputes or consumer matters and they don't have time to settle the consumer disputes before them amicably. Secondly, their normal procedure will not permit such huge deviation.

PROCEDURE

In West Bengal, mediation is a regular institution or mechanism to settle consumer disputes under the Consumer Affairs Department through the Directorate of Consumer Affairs and Fair Business Practices. There are officers deputed in every Forum and the State Commission who will take up the mediation at the instruction of the Presiding Officer of the Forum or the State Commission or at the behest of any of the party. On receipt of the petition, the officer of the designation of Consumer Welfare Officer gives notice to the other party inviting him on the date fixed to the mediation table for settlement of dispute.

On the date fixed, he conducts preliminary hearing and decides to call both parties on a convenient date to arrive at a settlement. On the fixed date and time, he sits in a free and open atmosphere so that parties can negotiate without preconceived notions or their rigid stands.

Firstly, he sits in a room which is free from disturbances. He starts the mediation after their preliminary introduction. Then the Petitioner presents his case with detailed facts. Mediator elaborates the facts with which opposite party may not be aware of. The opposite party gives his reply. Then the mediator chalks out points for discussion. He briefly outlines the points of consideration of the consensus. Then he clarifies the stand of every party as per the provisions of the Consumer Protection Act, 1986. Afterwards, he allows elaborate discussion on points settled *i.e.* examination, cross-examination, arguments and counter arguments all together.

The parties may be emotionally surcharged at this stage. In that situation, he takes the assistance of an outsider including some psychologist, if possible. He sits with each party separately. Then he arranges their joint meeting. After their consent, a joint draft is prepared and is discussed again and weighed in the light of the relevant provisions of the Consumer Protection Act, Rules and Regulations. When it is agreed upon and signed by both the parties in his presence, it is referred for implementation.

PERFORMANCE

About 3500 disputes have been settled in West Bengal out of about 5000 disputes filed with various mediation officers or otherwise in the State by the year 2009. The process is going on successfully. This is the most successful wing of the Consumer Affairs Department. Many letters of appreciation are received by the Department for the services rendered by the Mediation Officers with the State if any of the party does not agree, he is free to go to the Forum in regular course. To be successful mediator, the mediator has to put himself into the shoes of both parties. He should have sufficient knowledge of consumer laws and procedure to bind parties. For this purpose training is required for officers in the government set up so that they can forget their government hat of power and work for amicable settlement in a free and relaxed manner.

In USA and in Europe, most of the consumer disputes are settled by way of mediation by NGOs, VCOs or the Advice Centres. They charge fees also and are functioning very successfully.

CONCLUSIONS

Times are not far when mediation will be accepted as a legitimate tool in India in the field of resolution of consumer disputes and will be implemented with free help, patronage and support of the Central and State Governments. It is expected that it will find specific mention in the rules under the Consumer Protection Act, 1986.

◆◆◆

38

ADR at Grass Root Level: the Madhya Pradesh Experiment

The Government of Madhya Pradesh has implemented the system of Nyaya Panchayat in Madhya Pradesh. There is Nyaya Panchayat at each Block or Panchayat Samity Level. This Nyaya Panchayat is constituted separately from the block Panchayat or Panchayat Samiti. It has the local members who are generally well versed in law or are local respected elder persons. Generally, legal professionals including retired judges who are living within the block or the Panchayat Samity are the members. There are generally 7 to 8 members in each Nyaya Panchayat. Some of them are local lawyers also. They are sitting on fix days in a week preferably for 2 days in a week. The cases are filed with the Peshkar of the Nyaya Panchayat, who is one of the functionaries of the panchayat bodies. Sitting of Nyaya Panchayat is taking place in the office of the Gram Panchayat and the secretary of the Gram Panchayat was looking after the filing of the cases with the Nyaya Panchayat also. At some other places, they are exclusively tagged with the Nyaya Panchayat. There are no formal procedures. Parties can file petitions & replies on plain papers. They can place their cases or can take somebody else to place on their behalf.

I visited two or three Nyaya Panchayats in District Seoni, Madhya Pradesh during April 2004. These Nyaya Panchayats mostly reconcile matters before them and are imposing fines up to ₹ 500/-. Convicted parties mostly pay the fines as per the decisions of the block Nyaya Panchayats. Among the disposed of cases, I found that 60% cases were amicably settled or reconciled between the disputants. In case of 20%, the fines were imposed and paid. In case of other 20% cases, parties didn't agree and went to the regular Courts in appeal or as fresh matters. It was found that the judgments of these Nyaya Panchayats did not restrict the parties from going to District Courts. The Nyaya Panchayats were generally disposing of cases *of* petty nature, which are as follows;

(i) Cases, of diverting the water channel from one field to another field,

(ii) Cases of theft of crops,

(iii) Cases of altercation or assault on neighbours,

(iv) Disputes arising for drinking water,

(v) Dispute arising due to illicit relations,

(vi) Cases regarding petty money transactions,

(vii) Cases of petty thefts like theft of bicycle etc.,

(viii) Case regarding encroachment or trespass of lands or on built up area.

(ix) Dispute regarding payment of land revenue and other taxes by the local bodies.

(x) Cases of minor accidents,

(xi) Case of cutting of trees and bushes from forests or from private lands and

(xii) Cases of domestic violence or marital disputes not amounting to divorce.

It was found on the field visit that the system of disposal of cases by block Nyaya Panchayat was very popular among the people and is a very well established system of Nyaya Panchayat throughout the State of M.P. Nobody criticized the system as because legal expertise was also available on the bench. But it was found that the cases were also piling up because reports were not forthcoming from local level revenue officials like *patwari* or *lekhpal* and others regarding land disputes. Land disputes could not be settled without the intervention of local revenue machinery by demarcation of land which had the great salutary effect on settlement of disputes. However no case was pending in the Nyaya Panchayat for more than six months.

Small honorarium was paid to the members. They were happy as because many of them were retired govt, employees and sat on the bench as a matter of social service.

It cannot be said that this block Nyaya Panchayats were not following legal norms. In fact, most of the cases disposed of by them were found conforming to the statutory provisions and procedures of major Acts or statutes of the country, which are contained mainly in Code of Civil Procedure, Code of Criminal Procedure and the Indian Penal Code.

The experiment is hailed as a success at the grass root level.

◆◆◆

> *If a nation could not prosper without the enjoyment of perfect liberty and perfect justice, there is not in the world a nation which could ever have prospered.*
>
> **– Adam Smith**

39

How much Protection is Available to Judges and Magistrates?

Section 197 of the CrPC says "When any person who is or was a Judge or Magistrate or a public servant...accused of any offence. alleged to have been committed by him in the discharge of his official duty, no Court shall take cognizance of such offence except with the previous sanction."

The corruption in the lower judiciary has become a matter of public concern. People visit courts everyday and find lot of complaints of corruption against the exalted seats of justice in India.

This debate has now assumed importance, especially when the Supreme Court has held that there can be no discrimination between a Joint Secretary, Government of India, and other public servants and there is no requirement of sanction to prosecute a public servant. A retired public servant can even be prosecuted after many years of his retirement for the acts or omissions done by him during his service without proving *mens rea* for any crime committed by him, including corruption or negligence. This puts him on a lower pedestal than an ordinary person for crime. Though Judges do not find mention in various judgments of the Apex Court, yet it is presumed that the Judges can be similarly prosecuted without any sanction as they are also public servants.

However, the presumption cannot be so simplified as the Judges (Protection) Act, 1985 comes in the way as a special law.

This is a one page Act but is an improvement over the earlier law *i.e.* the Judicial Officers' Protection Act, 1850 after considering the 104th Report of the Law Commission of India submitted on 10th October, 1984. The Act provided a blanket protection to Judges and Magistrates by way of the clause: "No Court shall entertain or continue any civil or criminal proceeding against any person who is or was a Judge for any act, thing or was a Judge for any act, thing or word committed, done or spoken by him when, or in the course of, acting or purporting to act in the discharge of his official or judicial duty or function. However, the Central Government, or the State Government or the Supreme Court or any High Court or any authority under any law can take action including departmental proceedings."

EXEMPTION FROM CIVIL COURT ONLY

But no criminal action is reportedly taken against any Judge or Magistrate worth mention even in the infamous Ghaziabad District Court Provident Fund scam case whereas thousands of Government servants have been prosecuted and lodged in jail from the lowest level to the highest level except some wholesale dismissals of Judges and Magistrates for their gross dereliction of duties. The Law Commission only recommended exemption from Civil Court proceedings for anything done in good faith. One fails to understand why Parliament had specially exempted the Judges and Magistrates from criminal liability. This exemption to Judges has to be considered along with the provisions contained in the Judges (Inquiry) Act, 1968 and a plethora of judgments on the issue.

In *Delhi Judicial Service Association* Vs *State of Gujarat,* the three Judge Bench of the Supreme Court held that the judicial officers shall not be taken to a police station without the prior order or direction of the District and Sessions Judge of the concerned district, if available.

It is high time that the legal protection to Judges and Magistrates is reviewed in view of the multifarious complaints of corruption pending against them in the setup of various High

Courts to tone up the judicial administration, and to liquidate a huge pendency of more than two crore cases in subordinate courts. But adequate security has to be provided to Judges and Magistrates who decide cases against antisocial elements, gangsters, members of the mafia and other such persons. India does not have the environment like in Australia where Judges travel in public transport and share residences in public colonies. At the same time corruption by the ministerial staff of courts has gone beyond limits which was recommended to be curbed by the 104th Report of the Law Commission.

In view of the alleged increasing corruption in the lower judiciary, the latest decisions of the Apex Court on liability under Section 197 of the CrPC and the ineffectiveness of vigilance cells of various High Courts, it is the time to reconsider the 104th Report of the Law Commission by making suitable amendments in the Judges (Protection) Act, 1985.

1–15, October, 2016, Bureaucracy Today

♦♦♦

LAND REFORM

40

The Chinese Revolution to Implement Land Reforms

Distribution of land and property has been the mainstay of the human race since its origin. It was at the heart of the Prophet of Islam, the Roman Empire and the Chinese dynasties. Inequity has never been an acceptable principle of the human race but inequity continuously flourished in societies.

In China, the process of consolidation started with the setting up of the Kuomintang leadership but the political, judicial and economic power in the countryside continued in the hands of the land owning class and its intermediaries. In the matters most directly affecting the peasants - like the administration of their villages or the amount of taxes they had to pay - the Kuomintang could enforce neither efficiency nor justice. Growth of population, the declining individual share of cultivable land, its unequal distribution, high rents and still higher interest rates collected by the money-lenders, maintained the majority of peasants as prisoners of an informal cycle barely above the subsistence level, without any margin of safety. Drought or flood brought tragedy. Exorbitant rents and interest rates spread insecurity and that merely helped to drive interest rates and rents still higher. Yet after a bad harvest the farmer was driven to the money-lender, to place his land under mortgage and to accept such high interest rates that he would never finish paying off the loan and would ultimately lose his land.

All this, together with high taxation by local regimes, particularly in areas under warlords, put the majority of farmers under intolerable pressure. That dangerous explosive forces were thus created, or that change was needed, was generally admitted. But how to proceed was less easy to decide. Some of the more farsighted counsellors of the Kuomintang were urging the government to act. But political power was in the hands of the landlords who were often also the money lenders. Even the most generous compensatory scheme would have been against their immediate interests. Yet in the early 1930s, there was some hesitation in view of the urgency of the problem. At one stage a pilot scheme was envisaged in the province of Kiangsi to try out agrarian reform on a limited scale. In 1934 a group of experts of the League of Nations were invited to help draw up the detailed land reform programme. But this, as many other projects of a similar nature, never got beyond the stage of intentions.

Instead, the more convenient method was resorted to of passing apparently satisfactory legislation which was never seriously enforced. This way a law was passed ordering the lowering of farm rents to 37.5% of the crop yield, and the abolition of subtenancy and the right of perpetual lease. It remained on paper. The landlords continued to collect rents going from a half to over two thirds of the harvest. Interest rates were never controlled and there was no alternative cheap rural credit. Not infrequently, after payment of his rent, his interest rates and of his taxes, the cultivator was left with no more than a 50%, or perhaps even less, of the fruit of his labour.

Evidently, injustice on such a monumental scale could not be lasting. But there was no philosophy or theory of reform to inspire change. Nationalism alone was not enough. Chiangkai-Shek's overestimation of the importance of financial power as the expression of the established order went together with indifference to public opinion or to the need for reform and social change. And that obsession accompanied him like a shadow from canton to the Shanghai massacres, and from his alliance with the bankers and industrialists right to the strategic conception of the wars he was to conduct. As a reaction and influence of success of communism in Russia under Stalin, the Chinese Red Army emerged as the Communist military force. The communists organized insurrections in the countryside.

Mao Tse-Tung had been sent to his native Hunan province to organize peasant disturbance there. He was chased and he withdrew to the mountainous border. At the same time, PengPai managed to form a peasant militia and to establish the first Chinese Soviet Government in the sparsely populated Haifeng and Lafeng areas not far away. Throughout the scattered rural Soviets, Chinese communism was beginning to acquire a modest territorial base. The small Red Armies adopted guerilla tactics and they started getting conquests. Mao Tse-Tung emerged as the foremost leader. The Shanghai Control Committee couldn't overlook or brush aside the emergence of Mao Zedong in spite of their reservations.

In 1931 November, Mao Tse-Tung was chosen as uncontested leader, the first Chairman of the 'Provisional Government Born in 1893. He was one of the four sons of a peasant. Later, he founded the Chinese Communist Party at Peking at the age of twenty eight. He carried popular quotations and colourful images which sprinkle his writings and speeches and which provided him with a natural bridge to the minds of the Chinese people. He made a passionate plea: "The force for the peasantry is like that of the raging winds and driving rain. It is rapidly increasing in violence. No force can stand in its way. The peasantry will tear apart all nets which bind it and hasten along the road to liberation. They will bury beneath them all forces of imperialism, militarism, corrupt officialdom, village bosses and evil gentry. The democratic forces in the village have arisen to overthrow the feudal forces in the village."

He convinced every one that unlike in Marxism, the peasantry was not the reactionary force. He established the peasantry's role as the main force of revolution. He knew that no Chinese peasant rising had ever succeeded without leadership by the scholars - officials. The Kuomintang's police and armed might under Chiangkai-Shek couldn't make much headway against the rebel communist regime as their forces receded and dissolved before the attacker, only to re-appear in some fresh sector of armed strength. Corruption was threatening the vitals of the regime like a cancerous growth. The highest dignitaries were turning to profiteering and graft and were amassing fortunes.

While most people had to put up with great hardships and suffered from shortages of even essential goods, members of the government and high officials lived in safety and in comfort, thereby further contributing to the sagging morale of the population as a whole. The communists were steadily extending their influence and rivalry was increasing for power between them and the Kuomintang. The Red Army was incorporated partially into the Nationalist armies, received a monetary subsidy as well as a small allotment of ammunition. Mr. Chou En-Lai was recognized as their principal delegate in the capital.

Even after the Japanese had overrun many areas, they couldn't occupy more than the big cities and the main lines of communications. The Policy of the communists was to infiltrate into these regions and to set up local administrations within them through guerilla units. The Kiangsi method of the expropriation of landlords now gave way to a more selective process whereby only the absentee landlords' holdings were confiscated while in the case of cultivating landowners, only rents were reduced by the reduction of the proportion of the crop they exacted from the sharecroppers. Similarly, rather than to abolish debts, interest rates were controlled. The expropriated land among the landless were redistributed among the landless, by the organizations of local Soviets, Councils or rural co-operatives.

Thus with the energies and enthusiasm generated in villages, the original Shensi army of 30,000 men in 1935 developed into a force of one million, composed mainly of peasants, and supported by a militia of nearly twice that size. In 1940, Mao Tse-tung's essay On New Democracy established a new Marxist-Leninist theory which based revolution on peasants rather than industrial workers. He even admitted small landowners and nationalist capitalists to the broad national front. The Americans, being great supporter of democracy around the world didn't support Kuomintang as Mao Tse-tung was leading China to a people's democracy.

In 1948, the major Nationalist garrisons, containing the government's best armies had been isolated. The Communists closed in on Manchuria and established its hold. Mukden and other big cities surrendered gradually. Within four and half months from the beginning of the Manchurian collapse to the occupation of Peking, the Nationalist armies had lost over a million men. Most of them defected to the communists, taking with them over half a million rifles and huge quantities of other modern equipments, most of it American.

Flushed with success and with complete victory within sight, there was a significant shift in communist propaganda. On 21

January, 1949, the General Issimo announced his decision to withdraw. Chiangkai-Shek fled and took refuge on the island of Formosa . On 21st October, 1949, Mao Tse-tung, proclaimed the People's Republic of China and became the first Chairman of the Republic. This was the end of the Chinese Revolution but was the beginning of implementation of land reforms by the new communist regime.

However, taking the clue from the peasants' revolution of China, there were many conflicts and agitations around the world and there are still many movements including violent ones are going on. One of these is Naxalism movement in India. The Naxalite agitation still couldn't succeed because the State is very powerful now-a-days with very sophisticated weapons. As a result, the revolutionaries take refuge in jungles or forests and are unable to show their bonafide by even symbolic achievements to the suffering peasantry and they only indulge in guerrilla warfare against the salaried armed forces who are sent to fight against them without much of moral or motivation dose. Thus, these movements are only playing hide and seek games with no results forthcoming for the teeming millions.

In the process, the main issue of implementation of land reforms including equitable distribution of land goes in oblivion. There are many lessons to be learnt from the Great Chinese Revolution so that land may become conduit to reduce poverty in the society.

This was also done successfully in Brazil through the Rural Landless Workers' Movement (MST) within the ambit of the Constitution of Brazil. The militant members used to enter the property or land late at night, and they erected, temporary barracks out of heavy plastic sheets and woods Then the negotiation with landowners and Government would go on and off. Even unproductive land was also included for expropriation and distribution among the landless squatters to fulfil the 'social function'.

The initial phase of China's high and sustained growth and poverty reduction spurt clearly was linked to its 1979 change from collective large scale farms to small family farms. When collective production was abandoned and key agricultural markets were liberalized, China's peasant sector initiated rapid economic growth that dramatically reduced poverty. Equity in land distribution is associated also with overall high economic growth. Thus, China's successful land reform story proves that the Indian model of land reform is sustainable and can bring about prosperity in the society.

1-15, October 2014, Business Economics

◆◆◆

41

Land Distribution as a Tool of Poverty Reduction

The equitable distribution of land will ensure a peaceful foundation of the polity on which any industrialization or technological advancement can take off without any turmoil in future. No country can depend on uncertain import of foodgrains during crises like external and internal conflicts, especially during globalization where market forces are ruling-the roost. On the other hand, it will not be an exaggeration to state that Pakistan was dismembered into Pakistan and Bangladesh because the Pakistani dictatorial rulers enhanced the ceiling limit in Bangladesh up to 120 acres to woo the middle class and, big 'landlords.' The United Nations' Fourth Report (1970) says that "the redistribution of land can lead to the spread of national consciousness, which is a pre-condition for popular national government."

Re-distribution Programmes Implemented

Broader entitlement approaches commonly used to redistribute land to the landless and the 'land poor' have been introduced in many countries including Brazil, Kenya, Malawi, Namibia, the Philippines, South Africa and Zimbabwe. In some countries like Brazil and Zimbabwe, programmes targeting different groups are run simultaneously. In other countries, such as South Africa and India, a single programme is designed to benefit various groups. Albania and the Commonwealth of Independent States countries opted for distributing land to the workers. Most countries in central and eastern Europe and the Baltic States took the restitution route, whereas Hungary and Romania used a mixed strategy. A ceiling capping the quantum of land one can own is often defined by law, and all agricultural land above the ceiling that is rented out or has been occupied peacefully for a long time is targeted for distribution like in Brazil, Columbia, India, and the Philippines. Brazilian and Columbian programmes also focus on underused or poorly used land, partly because land is abundant and much of it is under-utilized. In Kenya and Zimbabwe, land re-distribution has focused on white-owned farms and exempted black owners from expropriation.

Another mechanism of land acquisition is outright confiscation or seizure of land for the poor and the landless. This occurred as revolutionary land reforms were undertaken in France, Russia, Eastern Europe, China, Cuba and other communist countries. Extreme rural poverty had virtually been eliminated in Cuba after the land reforms. Australia, Canada, New Zealand and the United States have introduced land restitution schemes either to restitute property or to provide fair compensation to individuals or communities unfairly dispossessed.

The state's role in land re-distribution is very important. Even after forcible occupation of land of large landholders, the state has to recognize and protect the possession by the poor of the land. But in the state itself, there are some conscious bureaucrats and political executives who have successfully implemented re-distribution programmes of land in their limited sphere of influence. Political parties also played important roles. Regimes, which came to power as a result of political upheavals like in independent India, Mexico, Bolivia, Nicaragua, Cuba, China and Vietnam had a mandate to implement land redistribution measures, and they did a bit from their end. As long as the slogan of land distribution helps them more than anything to win votes, they will adopt the same tactics. International organizations like the World Bank, the FAO and the ILO promoted land re-distribution programmes. Progressive NGOs and international organizations can play important roles as catalysts in helping grassroots peasants and landless movements to organize and press their demands for lands. In India, one political cum saintly leader Vinoba Bhave collected lakhs of hectares land in donation and distributed these among the landless and those who needed it the most to cultivate the land personally.

There are many advantages of the land redistribution programme. For rural households, land is an effective instrument to accumulate wealth and to transfer wealth to the next generation. Land ownership is a source of self insurance and old-age and all weather social security. Land can be sold, rented out, or pawned for consumption smoothly in response to shocks and life cycle stages. Further, land ownership is a source of security in continued access to the same plot of land, offering the possibility of capitalizing on long term investments and a source of local social capital and credit from banks and other financial institutions or local moneylenders. Land ownership is also a source of social status and bargaining power.

Feasibility of Land Redistribution Programme in Urban Areas

The guiding principle as per the Constitution of India for distributive equity in landed properties in rural and urban areas is that "the ownership and control of the material resources of the community are so distributed as best to serve the common good and the operation of the economic system does not result in the concentration of wealth and means of production to the common detriment." To achieve this purpose, no person in an urban area should be entitled to hold urban land in urban and urban agglomerations beyond a limit. Private dealing in urban land in recent years led to much speculation and profiteering. It has also been noticed in recent years that large palatial buildings with show of luxury have come up on extensive areas comprised therein. None can justify the building of a large villa by industrialist Laxmi Mittal in London for more than USD 100 million and by celebrities like football player David Beckham for USD 50 million.

This is not good for a stable society. On the other hand, every citizen has a right to a residential plot of land or at least a residence. It is attractive from an equity perspective but is difficult to apply because land is not available. Thus squatting is encouraged. It is therefore imperative that the urban poor are at least given shelters so that they can earn their living without an assurance of some physical security. The urban poor are more interested in finding a job rather than finding a plot whereas in rural areas, land is the only way for livelihood and to protect the poor from starvation or hunger.

The urban poor enjoy a better life because poor slums are adjacent to rich neighborhoods and they find easy jobs in the domestic chores of the rich people. The farthest out are squatter settlements; they are next to the poorest groups but not the poorest. The poorest live in slums or even sleep on the streets as in Kolkata. The rich occupy the areas with the highest amenities. Good scenic areas, access, locations with good views etc. are occupied by the high income groups. The poor are relegated to the most inhospitable terrain like steep slopes and marshes. Their primary interest is in land as shelter and security. Even then, the last two decades have seen an explosive growth in the size of cities in almost all developing countries. This growth can in large measure be attributed to rural-urban migration reacting to the poor condition in the countryside or expectation of higher income in the city. Therefore, there has to be an expansion of the supply of urban land and more intensive use of existing land. While the supply of all land is not like rubber which can be stretched, the supply of urban land can be stretched. Conversion of rural land to urban use, release of undeveloped lands in urban areas or better use of public land and housing or accommodation of more people in a given space constitute increases in the effective supply of urban land.

Much more is being done by the private builders than the government agencies or authorities. In cities, there is no other alternative except to arrange large scale housing facilities for the urban poor. An experiment was done in India by enforcing the Urban Land (Ceiling and Regulation) Act, 1976 on the pattern of acquisition of land through ceiling in rural areas. However, the Act failed to achieve its purpose.

It is clear that land redistribution will 'certainly save the rural poor who are also land poor or the landless from starvation. After allocation of land at least for their subsistence, the responsibility is shifted to them to work hard on mother earth and earn their livelihood. The state's responsibility to the extent of keeping them away from hunger will be over. However, this solution is not effective in the same way in urban areas. In urban areas, more important issues are employment and housing. But in every house allotted, the urban poor should have proportionate ownership of land in group housing.

The title of land or house would enable the allottees to access the credit market. Then, they can themselves try to come out of poverty traps. The poor fail to get out of poverty not because they are unproductive or lack skills, but because, due to credit market imperfections, they never get the opportunity to utilize their innate ability. However, neither the rural poor nor the urban poor should be allowed to sell off such assets allotted to them by the government or state or by the community because the poor have an unlimited number of problems which are equally very pressing. To safeguard them from temptation of either mortgaging or orally handing over the possession of their land asset, they should have social and personal security and insurance at least against serious diseases or lethal ailments if not against crop failure. In any way, the redistribution of land or urban housing is a great step forward to alleviate poverty from mother earth.

1–15 July 2014, Business Economics

♦♦♦

What is necessary for the use of land is not its private ownership, but the security of improvements. It is not necessary to say to a man, 'this land is yours', in order to induce him to cultivate or improve it. It is only necessary to say him, 'whatever your labour or capital produces on this land shall be yours'. Give a man security that he may reap, and he will sow.

– Henry George

42

Organising the Unorganised

In India, there were a number of movements to get rights to the land poor. After independence, zamindari was abolished and surplus land was distributed to the landless or marginal farmers. Author writes that these government lands can be enjoyed by the land poor only if their rights are protected against the organised onslaught by the erstwhile Zamindar or landowners.

Karl Marx has termed 'madness' of patience among farmers, unlike industrial labourers who are conscious of their rights and have basic infrastructure and tenacity to organise themselves against exploitation. In India, the Himalayan patience of the farmers against the exploitation negatives the thesis of agrarian revolution to a large extent. The very psyche of the cultivator is perhaps one of the subdued nature.

No society, has ever substantially reformed itself by a movement from above. As a matter of fact, the agrarian labour, as pointed by the International Labour Organisation, must be treated with preference but our labour laws only, cater to needs of the organised (except the Minimum Wages Act,) and their associations are strong to deal with the state and the employers. Here employers are also easily identifiable. But in agrarian field, both are unorganised and the state remain as "onlookers". The scattered nature of agricultural workers, their personal contact with and the dependence on the landlord, lack of group cohesiveness arising out of diverse culture, religions or castes and wasn't of identical goals. Lack of any permanent works status with any particular employer, their small proportion to the number of employers, and the substitutability of hired labour by family labour are some of the constraints that come in the way of organising rural labour, according to G. Myrdel. Swedish Nobel laureate and economist.

INTERNATIONAL SCENARIO

Article 39 of the USSR Constitution (1977), also ensured that enjoyment by citizens of their rights and freedoms shall not be the detriment of the interests of society and state of infringe the rights of other citizens. In erstwhile USSR, co-operative farming was largely successful until the USSR had a jolt of change of system from Soviet Republics to Commonwealth of Independent States in 1991. In Eastern Germany too, after the reunification of Germany in 1990, the large farms are left without help.

Mao Tse - Tung imposed a Marxist solution during the Great Cultural Blood Revolution (1949), in which about 25 million people were killed. He distributed 300 million acres of land among 400 million people and then collectivised the land. The modern development of China is now solidly based on successful redistribution of land whereas most of the surplus government land has been distributed among 97 percent landless persons. In many countries, there were protracted and violent struggles. In Colombia, violence has been a focal point since the late 1930s. The temporal link between unequal access to land and open conflict may not be immediate cause. But failure to address them can significantly increase the potential for conflict like in the case of South Africa and Zimbabwe, where some groups have historically been deprived of their land rights.

Initially Christian missionaries organised the poor around land but they could not sustain long.

In South Africa and Zimbabwe, it was anti-apartheid fight against eviction mainly from white commercial farmers. A recent study from Uganda fids that unresolved conflicts reduced output on a plot of land by more than 30 percent.

In West Africa, the younger generation, especially those unable to find non-agricultural employment, often competes for lands with the descendants of migrants and questions their parents giving away land cheaply to "foreigners", an issue that can easily spill over into intercommunity conflict with a potentially far-reaching impact.

In Rwanda during 1988-93, the build-up of land issue led to gradual increase in the potential conflict and provided the conditions that finally led to the outbreak of civil war in 1994, which culminate into the worst communal genocide after the Second World War.

Investigators have identified the lack of adequate mechanism for resolving conflicts or clarifying the nature of land transactions as prime reasons for continued ethnic cleavage in Ghana and Ivory Coast.

In Brazil, there were movements against large land owners who under used their properties. There were occupation of the Fezenda Annoni (1985) and other large scale land occupations. As a result of constant pressure on government, there was large scale land redistribution in Brazil.

In Kenya, there was Mau Mau Revolt (1952-60) against the ruling British colonial power. Through the movement was defeated yet there was limited land redistribution.

In the Philippines, there were numerous militant peasant organisations unified under the Peasant Movement of Philippines in 1985 such as United Nationalists Democratic Organisations which arose against Marcos administration. There was Epifanio de los Santos Uprising (1986), As a result, there was large scale land redistribution.

The rising recognition of the importance of good land governance at the political level is noticeable. For example, the African Union, whose heads of states agreed in 2009 to the framework and Guidelines for land Policy in Africa, has called for the development of benchmarks against which to measure country performance in terms of land governance (African Union, 2009).

THE INDIAN SCENARIO

There were famous rebellious in India like Chuar uprising. The Kol uprising, The Santhal Rebellion, Pagal Panthi Movement, Rising of the Ramosis, the Poligars uprising & Tebhaga movement in West Bengal. These organisation could not live long or bear fruits for long.

Then there were non-violent movements during freedom struggle to get rights to the land poor which were reflected in land laws after independence abolishing zamindari and land to the tiller or tenants or sharecroppers (bataidar) and surplus government land distributed to the landless or marginal farmers. However, these government lands can be enjoyed by the land poor properly if they are organised to protect their rights against the organised onslaught by the erstwhile Zamindar or landowners.

The peasants have been organised in Kerala and West Bengal at the grassroot level by the communist governments in power and they ensure that land reform beneficiates mainly their land and land rights through the power of their organizations. Krishak Samitis in both the States were very much organised and powerful that none can play with the rights of the land poor. In other states and at All India level, the peasants have been organised to further the interests of political parties as their strong vote bank through rhetoric only. However, persons like Rajagopala are still organising farmers without any party colour and successfully vent the problems of farmers before the governments.

Naxalites in India have also organised themselves in India for the cause of land poor but it is debatable whether they are fighting for the causes of the land poor or are engaged to protect their own armed organisations against the action of the state police power.

Apart from religious and social reforms in Tamilnadu and organising the rural youths through the Nehru Yuva Kendra organization of Govt. of India, the Panchayat System (PRIs) and Self Help Groups are doing good work in India. Now, the Panchayats can distribute government surplus land through their efforts as the subject of land is allotted to them by the Constitution of India. They have to take imitative but that is not coming forth at required pace.

A revolution is underway in India, sponsored by the government. Lakhs of social-mobilisation institutions or formal and informal groups known as Self-help Group (SHG) have grown up. A SHG is an informal voluntary association of poor people preferably from the same socio-economic background. The group enables its members to gain their identity as individuals and their combined capacity to arrange raw material for rural handicrafts and inputs for cultivation and their joint efforts for marketing of their produce. It provides them with a platform from where they can access banks and public services and spearhead changes that affect them as poor people. There are SHGs of 10-20 poor women in general (5-20 poor women in hilly or difficult areas) belonging to the same village and sharing a common socio-economic background.

These SHGs have brought many social changes like opposing drinking by their male counterparts and infusing reprisals against corrupt officials in some parts of India. Support from NGOs has also been solicited through government channel in increasing public co-operation, organization of beneficiaries, advancement of rural technology, arranging for buyer-sellers meets in big cities successfully through an open organisation called Council for Advancement of Peoples Action and Rural Technology (CAPART).

It is hoped that new sun will rise through SHGs in India when they will be successful in organising the farmers in utilising their barren lands by implementing small water harvesting schemes at their level jointly with farmers and by saving farmers from exploitation of market forces.

♦♦♦

43

Development Over Land

The dichotomy between industrial development and agricultural development has been a long-drawn challenge before the government when it comes to land acquisition. However, the State has to strike balance between the requirement of development of industries and basic needs of agriculture sector.

None denies predominant prerogative of the State under the power of eminent domain to acquire land for industrial purposes to give fillip to the economy of a country. It is a fact of the modern day world of globalisation that agriculture sector is gradually losing its edge as its share in GDP of a country is being continuously reduced. But one shouldn't overlook the fact that ultimately people will have to fall upon the agriculture sector to feed themselves. When globalisation or industrialisation doesn't perform, the agriculture sector being evergreen sector saves the humanity from famine irrespective of the economic cycle and its complicated calculations.

In developing and less developed countries (LDCs), in spite of reduction of share of agricultural sector in GDP, the percentage of population on agriculture is not being reduced in the same portion though urbanisation is the first brother of globalisation. Therefore, a balance is to be struck between the requirement of development of industries and services and basic needs of agriculture sector so that it always meets foods needs of the growing population of every country without considering the interstate movements of foodgrains which might be adversely affected during war, hostilities or civil strife.

MAKING AN EXCEPTION

It is therefore, essential that most productive agricultural land giving three crops in a year are spared from acquisition for industries and the persons dependent on agriculture are also protected so that this sector is always ready to fulfill the basic need of food of the population without which man cannot survive. The Voluntary Guidelines of FAO suggests that land banks should be set up to facilitate the acquisition of private land for such public projects, and to provide affected owners, farmers and small scale food producers with land in compensation that will allow them to continue and even increase production. Thus land, unfit for agriculture or low productivity lands either of public or private persons will be kept in each land banks and industrialists will be given choices only to choose among those parcels of land inspite of increase of overhead expenditure to them. Similarly, lands for environment protection or involving forests and fisheries will be tactfully spared from the acquisition or land except for emergencies like defence of country, natural calamities or for making basic amenities available to public like drinking water or water supply. But for these purposes too, only minimum feasible land should be made available to the public authorities.

THE WB EXAMPLE

In the present day scenario, the acquisition of land by the most powerful communist government of West Bengal ruling the State for more than thirty-years, was dethroned by the public. The land acquisition is the good trigger for public mobilisation as it is very obvious and the people have immediate fear of losing their livelihood. People have lost faith in industrialists as they feel that they are part of capitalist system which lives to serve itself more and more. The dichotomy between industrial development and agricultural development is best illustrated by following two cases, of land acquisition in West Bengal.

TATA MOTORS IN SINGUR

About 1000 acres of land was acquired by the West Bengal Industrial Development Corporation for the small car project of Tata Motors, in 2006. Tata is the most reputed industrial house in India. It was a privilege for West Bengal Government to host the plant of Tata small car project to manufacture ₹ 1 lakh dream car for the Indians. This was expected that with the arrival of Tata, other big industrial houses, and companies will follow suit in the industrial starved state of West Bengal, which had otherwise earned an ill-reputation of labour problems and lack of work culture.

Government of West Bengal decided to acquire land in record time for the Tatas on their conditions and provided them many concessions in land acquisitions costs, sales tax etc. The land was acquired without studying the pulse of local people and without the knowledge that it was the multiple cropping land and was one of the best for agricultural purposes in the State.

POLITICAL COERCION

While the land was acquired, the opposition in West Bengal opposed it tooth and nail saying that the farmers would not give away their lands as these lands were only sources of their livelihood. As a result, farmers of 234 acres of land out of 1000 acres (approx) did not accept the compensation amount. This became the cause of ever simmering discontentment. They formed an organisation under the banner 'Save Farm Land'. The supporters often disturbed the ongoing construction work and demolished the boundary wall many times. But the strong political will of the Government of West Bengal duly supported by Tata Motors, did not surrender to the demands of the local people to return back their fertile lands and instead using the land in front of the proposed unit which was less fertile.

The battle for the political supremacy had the unwanted consequences: One emerging young woman supporter of 'Save

Farm Land' was raped and murdered and this offence was committed at the instance of the local ruling CPM elite.

Then, there were cracks among the partners of the Left Front Government, which had been well cemented so far and has been ruling in West Bengal for more than thirty years.

There was a protracted court battle in the High Court of Calcutta through the Public Interest Litigation.

ON A STICKY GROUND

The problem of Singur attracted the world attention to the complex debate of land acquisition *vis-a-vis* development. If the local populace doesn't desire development, then why the development work is thrust on them. This also brought out the lax attitude of the West Bengal bureaucracy and the political elite who had been vouching as the only spokesman of the poor in the State. The development work was undertaken even without providing for a well laid down rehabilitation and resettlement policy even in the communist regime of the Left Front Government. Ultimately, Tatas withdrew from the project and have since vacated the site. Government of West Bengal has been left with no alternative.

The agitation against the setting up of the car manufacturing plant has cautioned the administrators and the policy makers that they should not take for granted the support of the poor. They are not only the deciders of their destiny. Their fate or progress has to be well chalked out in consultation with the local people at the grassroots level. Even elected panchayats or local-bodies cannot take for granted their support. The support is only issue based and election mandate does not give sole right to the elected representatives to speak or do everything on behalf of their electorates. The common people have no faith that they will be employed. They cannot support jobless growth. The land evictees should be trained in skills whereas they can get a job of their liking. The industrial house or management should provide jobs for the land-losers and should make provisions for due compensation considering development in the area as a result setting up of the industrial unit. The manufacturing unit should plan for people's needs and aspirations, to run the plant successfully in future. An unit cannot run smoothly without the support of the local people. These are the important lessons from the Singur land debacle.

CONTROLLING AGITATION

The case of Nandigram is an interesting one which brings out the fact, that apprehensions can also cause large scale public agitations and violence. Pursuing the declared policy of promotion of industries, Government of West Bengal had declared unofficially that there will be a chemical hub and other-housing projects near Haldia Industrial Centre under Haldia Development Authority. For that purpose, land will be acquired to the tune of more than 5000 acres. Rumours were having their sweep. In the meantime, the local MP being the most influential person, got published a pamphlet through a semi-Government organisation Haldia Development Authority that they would acquire land in 10-12 villages near Nandigram. This created panic among the villagers and they grouped under a non-political organisation known as 'Save Farm land Committee' irrespective, of party affiliation.

They even restricted entry of government officials to those 10-12 villages where the land was supposed to be acquired. They cut roads and put up barricades. Once, they were cutting Government pucca road, the police intervened. They stoned police force and in the melee, one police sub-inspector was killed and was thrown in the nearby Haldi river. The police force was sore about the incident and wanted to take revenge. Arrests on large scale were not possible because of resistance by about ten thousand people of the villages. Their anger was severe on CPI (M) supporters. As a result, the CPI (M) supporters were compelled to leave their houses. They took shelter in their nearby party bastion village Khajuri. All ten villages covering a population of about thirty thousand were united for one cause that the takeover of their land should be opposed at all costs even at the cost of their lives.

When a large police contingent under a senior officer of DIG rank went to arrest the culprits in earlier cases filed, the villagers started pelting stone and created obstacles on the roads leading to their villages. As a result, police resorted to bursting of tear gas shells and then firing as the crowd became uncontrolled and became very violent using bombs, grenades and arms against the police force. The ruling party supporters joined hands with police force and used brickbats, arms and bombs against members of 'Save Farmland Committee' which was locally known as 'Resistance Group against Land Eviction (Bhumi Uchhed Pratirodh Committee). In the melee, 16 people died including women who were opposing the land acquisition. Many policemen also got injured and were admitted in various hospitals.

END OF THE LINE

Cases of land acquisitions should be scrutinized closely by the higher echelon of administration and only minimum land required for the project should be allowed to be acquired. As far as possible, fertile agriculture land should not be acquired. If the industry or unit cannot be placed elsewhere, then alternative land should be arranged or offered for the cultivators to cultivate in nearby area out of the compensation paid to the land evictees. The people of the area should be heard properly before land acquisition plans are finalised. Land acquisition evictees should be given proper compensation even considering future increased value of the land due to industrialisation or development.

Land losers should be given jobs in the new unit as far as possible through a well represented body set up for the purpose. No land acquisition proposal should be cleared by the authorities unless it has proper rehabilitation and resettlement plan.

Thus, we should have a society with large sector of agricultural production that work in tandem with a certain kind of industry, rather than one is dominated by an abstract thing called industry - irrespective of whether it produces poison, nuclear hazards or automobiles. It is a misconception that in developing countries, private sector can replace the public sector in one go. It is to be softly done because the populace is not ready to absorb the reform, culture and are doubtful of the private sector due to their past history and practices. The South-East Asian countries had gone fast on private sector involvement and their economies were at the brink of collapse in nineties. On the other hand, China and India have been involving the private sector cautiously. Any reform without people's involvement will be lopsided. It is bound to fail ultimately. For example, uncontrolled land acquisition for industries is being opposed violently in India by masses specially for setting up of Special Economic Zones, because large manufacturing units are on fertile lands. The multinationals should not also be allowed to exploit raw materials of developing countries like India without ensuring improvement of quality of life of people. This type of development has become development terrorism. One cannot afford to have oasis in the poor neighbourhood. Equitable distribution is the only way out.

June 2014, Rural Connect

♦♦♦

44

A Milestone in SC Land Acquisition Judgments

The Supreme Court of India delivered an epoch-making judgment on August 31, 2016 in the case of land acquisition at Singur and other villages in West Bengal. The *Kedar Nath Yadav* Vs *State of West Bengal & Ors* case involved Tata Motors Ltd. The apex court has vividly interpreted the old and archaic Land Acquisition Act, 1894 in the light of changing times.

The Singur case judgment of the Supreme Court clearly lays down that land cannot be acquired for a private company unless "public purpose" is specifically declared. Even funds for acquisition should come from the public exchequer. In the Singur case, the land was notified for the Tata Motors Ltd company for its small car project which itself could not be termed "public purpose". The apex court said that it should be clearly spelt out that the project will be for socio-economic development, to generate employment and give fillip to the local economy. Secondly, the Court held that in cases of land acquisition, notices should be served to land owners individually which couldn't be established in the Singur case from the official records. However, it was not clear how a notice can be served to a person who is repeatedly refusing to get notice or the persons collectively who are obstructing to receive notices for land acquisition. Thirdly, the apex court clearly reiterated like in many previous judgments that proper opportunity of hearing should be provided by the Collector to the objectors of land acquisition. It will be more appropriate if the decisions on the disposing of objections are publicly published so that people may know why their objections were rejected by the Collector.

The Supreme Court further commented that the Tata Motors could not start operations as per the terms of the lease and farmers are entitled to take back their land and retain the compensation as they have been deprived of cultivation for the last 10 years. This includes the time taken in litigation at various stages.

The Tata Motors has also failed in concretizing the minimum land required for its plant generating employment for about 4,700 persons. Initially, the company wanted 700 acres of land and landed up taking 1,000 acres of land. As per the new Land Acquisition Act, 2013, the acquisition can be done for the minimum land required only. Thus, about Rs 611 crore went down the drain.

FAR-REACHING IMPACT

The Supreme Court's judgment will have a far-reaching impact on the implementation of the new land acquisition proposals with the Government. Now onwards land acquisition officers and decision-makers will have to be doubly cautious while implementing the provisions of the new Land Acquisition Act, They can no longer take shelter under the "sovereign functions and the power of eminent domain" for violations of due procedure under the Act. Secondly, the land for private entities will be acquired only in exceptional cases because they cannot provide compensation money from public funds. Additionally, they will have to provide for proper resettlement and rehabilitation packages before taking over the land. Thirdly, the projects having a commercial angle will also have to go through the process of social impact assessment. Fourthly, efforts will have to be made by the requiring bodies to avoid/minimize multi-cropped area or intensively cultivated land. The same provisions are also contained in the new Act.

Thus the Supreme Court's judgment in the Singur land acquisition case establishes that justice should not only be done, it should be seen to have been done. Justice should reach the deserving and deprived persons. The routine compliance with the provisions of law will not be adequate. It will be struck down by the ever vigilant apex court. It was, therefore, high time the administrative machinery in the land acquisition setup was geared up to face future challenges in land acquisition matters.

September 16-30, 2016, Bureaucracy Today

♦♦♦

45

Administrative Approach to Land Acquisition

It requires lot of administrative acumen, time-bound disposal of processes and co-operation among all agencies and Government departments to expedite land acquisition. Under the Rights to Fair Compensation and Transparency in Land Acquisition, Rehabilitation and Resettlement Act, 2013, proper steps are to be taken by the Land Requiring Body and the land acquisition wing of the Revenue Department of the State Government respectively.

The Land Requiring Body has to prepare a project report showing a public purpose, a total cost and the availability of funds, the period of project completion, a certificate that the land sought for acquisition is bare minimum and a proof of readiness for the placement of at least 80% of the funds with the Land Acquisition Department. For the purpose that the land required is minimum, national and international data for a similar project or industry is to be produced.

If a certificate from an expert is produced, it will facilitate the determination of the satisfaction of the Collector about the minimum requirement of land. In the case of Government or semi-government projects, a forwarding letter, from the Secretary or the head of a department is to be produced. In the past, many Government projects were delayed due to the non-availability of funds. Now there is no scope for the same as land acquisition officials are personally accountable for delay in land acquisition or in the payment of compensation.

In the case of private entities, the proof of availability, of full amount either through bank guarantee will have to be placed by them along with copies of updated records of rights or *khasras* of plots of land to be acquired.

The Land Requiring Body will also have to submit the Rehabilitation and Resettlement scheme if the land proposed to be acquired is equal to or more than one hundred acres. There is no exception to this provision after the amendment to the 2013 Act. However, the Collector has the power to quantify the Rehabilitation and Resettlement Scheme into a monetary amount which shall be administered by the Administrator. Therefore, there is nothing to be panicky about the land acquisition procedure.

If the proposal submitted is perfect in all respects as detailed above, the Collector will take permission for acquisition from the Secretary of the Department who in turn will go to the Cabinet if required. In the meantime, the Collector will update the land records of the affected areas. The Collector will notify the intention to acquire land for Social Impact Assessment purpose except in cases of projects relating to defence, rural infrastructure, affordable housing, industrial corridors, and infrastructure projects. After the approval of the appropriate authority, the Collector will publish a notification under Section 11 of the Act, 2013 and of which wide publicity will be given by him/her.

Any person can object to the notification within sixty days. The Collector will give an opportunity of hearing to the objector and dispose of the objections and submit his report to the Government giving the cost of land acquisition and the number of affected families likely to be settled for decision of the Government.

After approval by the Government, the Collector will publish the final notification for land acquisition in public interest and shall ask the Requiring Body (RB) to deposit the amount promptly not beyond one year from the publication of the preliminary notification.

Afterwards the Collector shall invite objections to taking possession of land, the claim of compensation and a rehabilitation and resettlement plan. The maximum time allowed to declare awards for the payment of compensation is one year after the final notification.

It is clear from the foregoing that no land acquisition proceeding should prolong beyond two years. But there is lot of floats provided at each stage. In an emergency situation, land acquisition should take six-seven months. However, if land acquisition proceedings are completed within a year, all concerned should be appreciated.

16–30, April 2015, Bureaucracy Today

♦♦♦

46

Land Reforms in Bangladesh

Before the formation of Bangladesh after its secession from Pakistan in 1971, there was a ceiling limit of 125 acres per family in Bangladesh against 12. 5 acres in adjoining West Bengal in India, which was once a part of united India before the partition of India in 1947. This obvious fallacy in agricultural land ceiling was because the dictators or elected rulers sitting in West Pakistan at a distance of more than thousand miles believed that if they can keep the rich peasantry or zamindars in good humour like the Englishmen, they will be able to keep their hold on the erstwhile East Pakistan (now Bangladesh) and perpetuate their exploitative regime. It didn't happen and Pakistan was dismembered. The leader of the Bangladesh Liberation Movement, Sheikh Mujibur Rahman, inter alia had promised to the masses that he will reduce the high ceiling limit on agricultural land and distribute government khas land among the landless poor. But the liberation leader was killed in the civil war before his promise could be fulfilled.

It is now left to the political leaders who came in or will come in power in the name of Bangabandhu. Most of the leaders who captured power by hook or crook had neither the requisite will nor the required political support to implement the major land reform measure relating to lowering of ceiling limit in Bangladesh so that surplus ceiling land vested in government can be distributed among the landless and land-poor cultivators who have been struggling in Bangladesh to meet both ends. The members of Sheikh Mujibur Rahman's family like his daughter Sheikh Hasina were threatened by the military junta or their cronies, the big landowners or zamindars. On the other hand. many land reforms were implemented in their friendly neighbouring country, *i.e.,* India. In 1977, the Left Front Government came to power in West Bengal, India, on the plank of implementation of land reforms, which were in the statute book but were not implemented in the field.

As the absolute majority State Government started implementing land reform measures like vesting and distribution of ceiling surplus land and recording of sharecroppers known as 'bargadars' and their benefits accrued to the teeming millions on the border, and the demand got generated for promulgation and implementation of land reform measures in Bangladesh which rulers could not overlook or resist.

In the meantime, a public conscious General H. M. Ershad came to power and he promulgated the Land Reforms Ordinance, 1984 on January 26, 1984. The tragedy is that so far that Ordinance could not be converted into an Act and is hailed as the *magna carta* of land reforms in Bangladesh.

REASONS AND OBJECTIVES OF THE ORDINANCE

The 1984 Ordinance was enforced to reform the law relating to land tenure, land holding and land transfer with a view to maximizing production and ensuring a better relationship between land owners and bargadars.

SALIENT FEATURES OF THE LAND ORDINANCE

The Ordinance inter alia recognized and protected the long prevailing institution of sharecroppers/ bargadars like in West Bengal in India as below:

"bargadar means a person who under the system generally known as adhi, barga or bhag cultivates the land of another person on condition of delivering a share of produce of such land to that person (as owner). "

However the provision regarding bargadar is an improvement over the West Bengal Land Reforms Act, 1955 as it provided the limitation of contract of barga cultivation only for five years whereas in West Bengal it is for lifetime and is heritable.

The Ordinance further prohibited eviction from homestead in rural areas. It was also a great step forward to protect the poor persons in rural Bangladesh.

The Ordinance also bars the jurisdiction of all courts against the decision, action or proceedings made or taken by any authority under this Ordinance.

STATUS OF IMPLEMENTATION OF LAND REFORMS IN BANGLADESH

The implementation of land reforms is not at a required pace. The revenue department, which is entrusted with the job, is still dominated by the bureaucracy from the landed class or middle class. They are more inclined to maintain the status quo than to create an atmosphere of conflicts in the society which they are not sure whether government in power will support. Secondly, pressure on land is very heavy in Bangladesh vis- a-vis other countries. The only best example before them is of the Left Front Government of West Bengal, which was in continuous power for more than thirty years on the main plank of implementation of land reform measures effectively. The present Government of Sheikh Hasina is a stable government, which has fought the religious fanatics decisively and has the requisite political will to ensure the right of rural poor regarding land. Let us hope that the present government takes up land reform issues more effectively rather than go for stopgap measures due to the protests by the people through NGOs. The government has launched a very successful scheme in Bangladesh of allotment of at least 16 decimal land for the three tier cultivation with the help of micro-finance after purchasing at the market rate from the willing land owners.

But the real job of allotment of khas land vested in the State to the landless or the land poor is still to take off as a mission along with the recording of bargadars as a special drive on the pattern of the neighbouring West Bengal.

NGOs are playing important role to organize the peasants for land reforms as leaders. Nijera Kori, Bangladesh Legal Aid and Service Trust (BLAST), Gonossha Hajjo Sangshta (GSS), and the Association of Land Reform and Development (ALRD) also provide valuable legal assistance to rural population. Nijera Kori is one of many non-governmental organizations which believes that the cause of poverty in Bangladesh is not the paucity of resources or over-population, rather unequal distribution of wealth and property mainly landed property. Nijera Kori considers title to khas land by the landless an integral part of poverty alleviation in rural areas. Firstly it is difficult to establish whether the land is one vested in government. Secondly, the powerful individuals try to grab government land. The landlords or landgrabbers bring false charges such as theft against the landless or the assignees of government khas land known as pattadars in Bangladesh. This makes it difficult for the landless or pattadars to have access to government ceiling or khas land, especially when they are not sufficiently organized and lack wider support. Nijera Kori has thus sought to organize the landless and to influence public opinion and government departments as well as legal support to its members involved in about 100 cases who were considered as the main foe by landlords and elites. Cases involved access to and formal tilling of khasland, land dispossession for shrimp cultivation, oppression of women, and sometimes murder charges to these issues. Nijera Kori was very successful in restoring, which had surfaced after receding the sea back water in two villages Char Bajja and Char Majid at Sundaram Police Station in Noakhali District of Bay of Bengal. There were many conflicts between the landlords and the settlers. Each of 200 settlers were allotted 1 acre of land to cultivate. Subsequently, these lands became very fertile and good for shrimp cultivation and attracted landowners, politicians, and local influential persons to usurp the land by hooks or crooks. Local administrators were called upon to undertake police assaults. Peasants' huts were burnt and crops were destroyed.

At the same time, law suits were brought against the peasants in the local and in the High Courts. In 1997, three persons were in jail serving life sentence, convicted in a bogus rape case. Without timely legal aid from Nijera Kori, the peasants would probably have been evicted from their land.

This represents the state of affairs of implementation of land reforms in Bangladesh.

CONCLUSIONS

It is clear that the NGOs are campaigning hard for land reforms. It is, therefore, more essential that the government takes initiative to implement land reform measures as per the Ordinance, 1984, which may be now made part of the statutes in force in Bangladesh. This will avoid uncertainty, unrest and violence in rural areas where in any case, the poor are uniting and exerting under some banner or the other. The governmental efforts will channelize their energies and steam off their grievances. The World Bank has also come up with a plan to revamp the land revenue or land reform set up of Bangladesh as a part of its latest move to remove poverty from the face of the earth through implementation of land reforms. World Bank can provide grant or even depute an agency to update land records of Bangladesh which is a pre-requirement to undertake extensive and permanent land reforms. The present government headed by Sheikh Hasina is a popular government, which has won its first battle against religious bigots in Bangladesh who do not allow such public oriented measures to be implemented to perpetuate their vested interest. It is hoped that the present government having the example of West Bengal, India before them will not hesitate to undertake land reforms measures immediately and extensively.

1–15, November, 2016, Bureaucracy Today

♦♦♦

47

Land Reforms in Pakistan

Pakistan is the sixth most heavily populated country in the world having an estimated population of about 20.5 crore people. Since the formation of Bangladesh, Pakistan has restructured its governance and economy.

Land reform is one of the areas which is directly linked with the amelioration of the conditions of the poor especially in countries like Pakistan that has a predominantly rural population. Land reform has been a provincial subject in Pakistan. Therefore, land reform statutes, legal provisions, and measures will differ from province to province. But in Pakistan, there is a marked uniformity except minor state or province specific variations because of a powerful central government.

Pakistan has an area of 310, 403 square miles and has four provinces, namely, Baluchistan, North West Frontier Province, Punjab, and Sind.

In 1972, under the Martial Law Regulation, 1959, steps were taken to abolish jagirs or estates without compensation. As a result, 2. 5 million acres of land were resumed and 2.3 million acres of land were distributed among only 183, 371 tenants and small land owners. This area constituted only 4. 5% to 5% of the total land in Pakistan.

The West Pakistan Land Commission found that the zamindars illegally changed land records in collusion with the revenue officials at the village level. The Land Reforms Regulation, 1972, the first enacted Regulation by the Pakistan People's Party government, prescribed a land ceiling of 150 acres of irrigated land and 300 acres of un-irrigated land or an area equal to 1500 PIUs. The ceiling limit itself was very high by any standard. The government resumed land without changing tenants and small owners, and redefined the contractual conditions between landlords and tenants including protection against eviction. This was the first positive step by law to protect the right of cultivation by the tenants-at-will *i.e.* share croppers who were cultivating lands of big zamindars on condition to share produce.

However, the land owners having big land holdings had the decision-making power in regard to selection of crops, use of inputs and such others. Even then, the sharecropper in Punjab and NWFP gets 60% share of the crop while in Sind they get 50%. The Act of 1972 provided that all tenants should be registered. No tenant or sharecropper can be evicted without his consent or unless he misuses his land. Personal cultivable, *i.e.*, Khudkasht area is up to 50 acres. This can be termed as Magna Carta to protect the rights of bonafide sharecroppers in Pakistan. Its due implementation can bring a new dawn to the tenants-at-will in Pakistan. This type of tenure is already in vogue in the tribal areas of Baluchistan and the NWFP.

The Land Reforms Ordinance, 1977 reduced the ceiling to 100 acres of irrigated land or 200 acres of unirrigated land. It is two thirds of the ceiling prescribed by The Land Reforms Regulation, 1972. The new Ordinance also allowed compensation to land owners in the form of bonds equivalent to ₹ 30 per PIU. An additional area of 1.8 million acres was resumed under the 1977 Ordinance of which 0.9 million acres were distributed among 13,143 persons whereas the number of land allottees should have been in millions.

INADEQUACY OF LAND REFORMS IN PAKISTAN

According to the census data for 1959, 1972, and 1980, land concentration as measured by the Gini Coefficient has remained unchanged over the years which were 0.62, 0.55 and 0.54 respectively. The land ownership concentration ratio varied from 0.64 in the 1950s to 0.55 in 1976. West Punjab is a land of peasant proprietors. There is a total of 13.5 lakh land owners in West Punjab. 9 lakh own land less than 5 acres, 11.3 lakh own land less than 10 acres while 1.8 lakh own between 10 and 50 acres. In NWFP, 47% land is held by large land owners. 42% land is directly cultivated by land owners whereas tenants with occupancy rights *i.e.* sharecroppers cultivate 11% land. The excess land in the N. W. F. P. and Baluchistan is more restricted than in the other provinces. This is also because of joint operations of individual holdings by tribal communities.

In economic terms, about 73. 6% of the Pakistani population is below the consumption level of $2 per day as per international standards. As per a report, the land records in Pakistan are not updated. The World Bank can assist Pakistan to update its land records like it has done for many other countries. Revenue courts are located at inconvenient places. The courts are dominated by judges from the landed class and critics opine that this can be the reason behind justice not flowing to the really affected people.

LACK OF POLITICAL WILL

Even the revenue bureaucracy is dominated by the personnel from the landed class. Therefore there is a deficit of administrative will. Political will and administrative will are two sides of the same coin. Thus, there is no political will to implement land reforms in Pakistan. Even Generals of the Pakistan Army are mostly from the landed classes in Pakistan.

LAND REFORM: A WAY OUT TO TACKLE EXTREMISM IN PAKISTAN

The windfall capital inflows from remittances from foreign nationals, of infrastructural inflows from China or foreign assistance from allies or all three combined cannot solve Pakistan's problems on a long term basis. Pakistan has to resort to structural reforms to reduce Pakistan's dependence on foreign aid and make Pakistan a stable and prosperous country. Such reforms can provide a strong alternative to the Islamic narrative and will and can tackle religious extremism.

SUGGESTIONS

It is now well established that like in West Bengal, India and Bangladesh, small parcels of land transferred to the new owners coupled with institutional or bank crop finance have generally had a positive impact on the levels of productivity and generate employment. It is therefore, essential that a much lower ceiling limit should be prescribed in Pakistan. Excess land even as per existing laws, regulations and ordinances should be resumed or vested by the government on payment of compensation with 4% interest. The excess or surplus ceiling land or resumed land need to be distributed in a democratic decentralized manner by involving local semi-government bodies like panchayats in India to the landless agriculture workers, sharecroppers or tenants. Land granted to fictitious tenants or ex-soldiers if not cultivated by him, should be resumed and a Benami Transactions (Prohibition) Act should be passed and implemented. Revenue Courts should be located at convenient locations so that they can deliver at the doorstep. All tenants or sharecroppers as provided in the Act of 1972, should be entered into Khata/Khasra or be registered. No tenant or sharecropper should be evicted without his consent, or unless he misuses his land and Khudkasht area or area under personal cultivation should be protected up to 50 acres as per the Act of 1972.

However, if a reform is to be carried out successfully, it must win the active support and ensure people's participation. Reform should run a little ahead of the social, economic and political situation of a country and should be connected with people.

1-15, May, 2017, Business Economics

♦♦♦

48

Status of Land Reforms in Nepal

Nepal is a land-locked central Himalayan country in South Asia located between China and India. The country is divided into seven provinces. It has about 25. 2% population living below the poverty line as per the 2011 estimates.

Land reforms had started in Nepal in 1951. An official policy issued in 1952 declared, "Unless the land tenure system is improved, the economic condition of the peasantry and agricultural production will not improve. Land ownership is passing from the hands of peasants to those of money-lenders and rich people but the actual cultivators do not have security of tenure. This has reduced agricultural production and increased the number of landless peasants. "

After 76 years, which included the rule of a Marxist government, the condition of the peasantry remains unchanged. The 1957 Lands Act granted the security of tenure to the tenants or sharecroppers but the measure was largely ineffective because of the lack of implementation at the local level and due to the lack of tenancy records. However, a major push to land reform measures was given in 1961 and 1964. In 1961, the panchayat system was introduced as local democratic administrative machinery, which apart from assisting in implementation of land reforms, was to supplement the supply of credit, fertilisers, and irrigation facilities, and facilitate the development of cooperatives. In 1964, a thrust on the twin objectives of land reforms, *i.e.,* ceiling on landholdings and distribution of government surplus land among the landless and rights to tenants or sharecoppers cultivating lands of others was given.

IMPLEMENTATION OF CEILING ON LANDHOLDINGS

The 1964 Lands Act prescribed a ceiling of 25 bighas of agricultural land for each family in Nepal. Land in excess of the prescribed ceiling was to be acquired by the government on payment of compensation which was fixed at ten times the land tax for agricultural lands. Nepal was divided in three regions namely Tarai and inner Tarai regions, Kathmandu Valley and Hill regions. By July 1972, the government of Nepal had acquired approximately 50,000 hectares of surplus land under this programme. This amounted to only 3% of the cultivated area. However, this performance was further cut down as only 22,000 hectares had been actually redistributed to around 10,000 families. This land could be distributed among many more families. This is one of the reasons why one finds so many Nepali workers in India and other countries. They neither have the land to work on nor the industries to be employed in.

The tourism industry has limitations and a villager can hardly be expected to be absorbed in it. The solution to this lies in completing land surveys, preparation of proper land records and in swift implementation of land reforms. Grants are available from the Word Bank and other UN agencies for land survey and for updating land records. On the other hand, many sophisticated technologies have been developed to simplify surveys in hilly and inaccessible terrain. The Nepal government's priority must be on distributing surplus land and then provision for credit and the co-operative farming under panchayats. However, for left out lands, public institution are now allowed to get govt. surplus land.

SECURITY OF TENURE TO SHARECROPPERS

As defined in the 1964 Lands Act, a tenant or a sharecropper is "a peasant who obtains land from a landowner on any condition and cultivates it through his personal labour or the labour of his family." In other words, actual cultivators were recognised as tenants or sharecroppers and intermediaries or Jimidars were abolished like the Zamindars in India. In 1961, it was estimated that 27.64% land was under tenancy. Out of the above, 35.01% land was irrigated and 16.85% was non-irrigated. This shows high incidence of sharecropping in Nepal. Tenancy is higher in Kathmandu Valley and Tarai regions than in the Hill region. In case of such lands known as the Raikar lands, 50% share of the produce was fixed to be given to the landlord and it grew as a custom. However sometimes, landowners even got two thirds of the gross produce of the main crop as share in hill districts including the Kathmandu Valley. It varied from two-thirds in the eastern Tarai to one third in the sparsely populated areas of the far western Tarai. In 1972, provisions related to sharecropping were applied to Raj Guthi lands. Tenants and sharecroppers were allowed to take bank credit for crop cultivation.

Eviction was permissible in the event of non-cultivation and non-payment of share or rent. The tenant cultivators were permitted to voluntarily relinquish their lands. But this provision was misused by landowners. Rana legislation correctly appreciated the problem of tenant cultivators and permitted tenant cultivators to redeem alienation of lands made in favour of others. It even provided to take preventive measure if the relinquishment was under compulsion of any kind. Thus, there is a clear spirit underlying the laws of Nepal to ensure security of tenure to the cultivator-tenants and sharecroppers. But in practice, due security of tenure is not available to the sharecroppers as the landlords are also moneylenders and the sharecroppers have to borrow money from them for cultivation who charge exorbitant rates of interest from the needy cultivators.

CONCLUSION

Religious sentiments in Nepal point to the fact that the cultivator should be allowed 50% share of crops in Guthi lands as the cultivator owes more allegiance to God. There is a need to revisit the limit of ceiling on landholdings as remnants of the Jagir system still exist. The Panchayats should be made more effective so that they can indirectly play a role in aiding community farming or cooperative farming.

Growth in the non-agricultural sector cannot be accelerated unless the primary sector of the economy which is agriculture is not restructured in Nepal. Benami land needs to be unearthed in Nepal and put for distribution among the landless or the land poor. A strong political will is required for this in addition to gearing up the revenue machinery. ?

16–31, August, 2017, Business Economics

◆◆◆

No man made the land. It is the original inheritance of the whole species. It appropriation is wholly a question of general expediency. When private property in land is not expedient, it is unjust. It is no hardship to any one to be excluded from what others have produced: they were not bound to produce it for his use, and he loses nothing by not sharing in what otherwise would not have existed at all. But it is some hardship to be born into the world and to find all nature's gifts previously engrossed, and no place left for the new-comer.

— John Stuart Mill

49

Suggestions to Remove Poverty in India

The eradication of poverty has been the main agenda of all Indian Governments since Independence. India has the largest number of persons in the world though it is estimated that their percentage to the total population of the country has come down from 30% to 25% or even 20%. The poverty line is based on a per capita daily intake of 2,400 calories in rural areas and 2.100 calories in urban areas. If we take the minimum per capita daily intake of 2,250 calories, a person will require 518 grams of foodgrains per day to eat.

Poverty reduction requires that the earnings of poor Indians should increase either through farm productivity or through income transfers as a result of implementation of governmental schemes. As per the latest approach of the World Bank, poverty is closely related to the availability of land with the farmer so that he may himself engage in cultivation and give his productivity to society. Land can also be made available for cultivation if the farmer's right of cultivation as a bataidar or bhagdar or bargadar *i.e.* as sharecropper is recognized and protected.

The Government has taken various steps to remove poverty in India. However, their proper impact could not be made as no Government is concentrating on solving the core problem of landlessness in rural areas. State governments are neglecting their solemn duty to distribute even surplus government land with them after implementing the ceiling law for agricultural holdings. They are paying no heed to the need for resolving the number of sharecroppers who are cultivating the land of others. As a result, there is no motivation in rural India to work hard and give optimum production. The Centre can financially assist State Governments to purchase land and distribute it among the landless or poor persons starting from the Naxal-affected areas.

Secondly, many of the small or marginal land owners are selling their precious land for special treatment of their kith and kin in private hospitals as proper treatment is not available in government hospitals. They are becoming new landless persons. The Government should provide them medical insurance at their doorstep like in West Bengal so that they do not swell the ranks of hungry people.

Thirdly, the Scheduled Castes and Scheduled Tribes's pattadars are allowed to sell their land to SCs or STs in the case of urgent need or distress. This land is ultimately purchased by rich people making them landless. As a matter of principle, patta land or government land is allotted by the Governor for the cultivation by the allottee or his family members and cannot be alienated by the assignee of vested land or pattadar. This relaxation of the rule should be done away with and the poor people should be supported by the Government in cases of dire needs.

Fourthly, banks are now mortgaging lot of land in rural India mainly against consumption loans such as for the marriage of daughters, for getting better medical treatment, purchasing motor cycles or bikes and getting education in private schools or in professional colleges or institutions. Thus banks are becoming new landlords in rural India. Many of these banks are serving the personal interests of local branch managers or staff. This pernicious practice should be stopped forthwith by the Government of India and loans to farmers should be given actually for cultivation purposes.

It is hoped that the Government will pay due attention to the above suggestions to make durable impact on the reduction of poverty in India.

1-13, May, 2017, Bureaucracy Today

♦♦♦

Poverty is the parent of revolution and crime.

— Aristotle

50

Removal of Poverty through Self Help Groups

A revolution is underway in India through lakhs of social-mobilization institutions or formal and informal groups known as Self-Help Groups (SHG). A SHG is an informal voluntary association of poor people preferably from the same socio-economic background. The group enables its members to gain their identity as individuals and their combined capacity to arrange for irrigation, seeds, fertilizers, and marketing. These groups can be formed to remove poverty in the agriculture sector.

The poorest of the poor in the majority of the Indian rural population are the pattadars (assignees of government vested land) and marginal and small farmers. They don't have their land as productive. Therefore, they don't have incentive to do cultivation. In India, the collective co-operative farming on the Russian or socialistic pattern cannot be implemented because owner of land even of small plot does not like to relinquish his or her ownership and pool in the collective co-operative farm. The ideal system for India is the Egyptian system. This is based on the individualistic model as distinct from a strictly collective co-operative farm where the government or its agent controls the ownership. This form will meet the basic instinct of the ownership of land of man which also motivates him to work harder even on cooperative or joint farm like loosely formed SHGs. He can at any time part with this formal or informal group. Within the group, the local Pradhan, Gram Panchayat can allow them to work under employment generating scheme like MGNREGA on their fields to create water resource like pond or wells by giving them daily wages to work on their fields and thus help them to form a SHG to share irrigation water and production among them. Combined or joint marketing of agricultural produce will protect them from exploitation by the middleman or market forces in urban as well as in rural areas. However, to operationalize such a SHG, the lands of members should be preferably adjoining or contiguous.

One such experiment was done in Andhra Pradesh, District Chittor through Kuraparthi Varipalle Gram Panchayat in Erragutta Block. Various activities under fallow land development *i.e.* jungle/bush clearance, stone bunding, slit application, trench cutting etc., were designed and executed along with rock filling dam works. As a result, the entire 45 hectares of barren land has turned into a well-developed mango-orchard. Each of the owner of land or member of SHG *i.e.* beneficiary derived income of about $200 viz ₹ 13,200/in the first year. Inter crops like groundnut, millets, watermelons, tomatoes etc., have also been taken up simultaneously. These provided an additional income $1500 *i.e.* ₹ 99000/ to each member of the SHG.

The scheme under MGNREGA has transformed lives of the poorest of the poor Scheduled Castes, Scheduled Tribes and marginal farmers by changing their status from agricultural labour to proud owners of orchards. This has also exploded the myth that so-called waste or barren lands cannot be distributed among the landless families as these lands are unfit of agriculture.

It is hoped that this type of innovation will pave way to remove poverty in rural India. If land is also provided to all landless, then the whole population of the poorest of the poor can be covered along with the allied activities like piggery, goatry or other dairy facilities. In this model, three layer cultivation on small parcels of land say 16 decimal and above can be promoted like in Bangladesh *i.e.* foodgrain crop on the ground, cash crop at middle level followed by high rise trees for industrial purpose. This model cannot be successful without linking it with macro finance viz crop finance on concessional interest rates or subsidy by the banks or other local level financial institutions or outlets.

In the foregoing model of development of small plots of land, not much efforts or support from the government are required. This can sustain on existing government schemes of employment generation which are always in vogue in one nomenclature or the other. It will be a relief to the poorest of the poor who are confused and fed up with multifarious slogans by the election candidates and by the successive governments at the Centre and States to remove poverty but they do not see much action or result on their ground and in their lives.

◆◆◆

> ***Man is guided by the stomach. He walks and the stomach goes first and the head afterwards...... It will take ages for the head to go first.***
>
> **– Swami Vivekanand**

GOOD GOVERNANCE

51

Tips for Good Governance

After the explosive victory of BJP leader Narendra Modi and the formation of his Government at the Centre, the issue of good governance has again come to the fore. Firstly, ministers and senior bureaucrats at the level of Secretary to the Government should not use official vehicles for sending their wards to schools or allow them to be used by their families or use their official telephones for personal purposes. Secondly, none of them should employ government peons, contingent employees or daily wage labourers at their official residences. If this is done by ministers and senior bureaucrats, the lower level officers and their staff will follow it sincerely. At present, the employment of daily wage labourers has become an unending process involving a huge outgo from the precious public exchequer. To pay to daily rated workers at the residence or in personal attendance of an officer, official records are manipulated. For this small favour, the officer loses control over his office and employees and he has to be a silent spectator to the vicious circle of corruption ending up to the last level of the hierarchy under him.

However, for ministers people still leave some latitude which will gradually evaporate in view of the growing public resentment against the working of the system at the top executive level. Thirdly, ministers have to be very cautious while visiting the field. At present if they want to enjoy free board and lodging at government guest houses, the District Collector has to arrange from some source or the other illegally. This causes a bad example at the field level and the District Collector loses the grip over his subordinates. Fourthly, ministers shouldn't use excessive security. Police officers increase the security guards of ministers gradually to please them by projecting the threat of security to their life or person. As a result, ministers are slowly cut off from the mainstream public and observe things as are fed to them by the police or their supporting bureaucrats or personal staff An objective assessment of security threat is not placed before them through proper channel. During the Jyoti Basu regime in West Bengal for more than 22 years, ministers didn't use government bungalows. They didn't have servants at their residences. Their party paid for their board and lodging at circuit houses or government guest houses. Even his Home Minister, Buddhadeb Bhattacharya, didn't carry a security guard with him. However, these things didn't benefit the Left Front Government during the 30 years of its continuous rule because its cadres at the grassroots had become corrupt and arrogant and ministers couldn't control them.

The present West Bengal Chief Minister, Mamata Banerjee, is also known for her simplicity and non-use of government facilities. The Kerala Government has been following the strict norms of financial discipline traditionally. The three-term Tripura Chief Minister, Manik Sarkar, has his total asset of about ₹ 11,000 only.

In northern Indian States, especially in UP, transfer and posting is the main thrust of ministers. After assuming power, they forget to implement their party programme or manifesto promised by them to the electorate. There should be a well-defined and published policy of transfer and posting at every rung of the Government under overall orders from the top. Even the Central Government doesn't have a well-published policy of transfer and posting. In the case of seniormost bureaucrats i.e. the Chief Secretary or Secretaries, there should be an independent board to recommend their transfers and postings. This was also directed by the Supreme Court recently and has been suggested by many committees or commissions set up for administrative reforms. Thus, the transfers and postings as the main sway of political executives should be stopped forthwith as this is the breeding ground of corruption and has put all measures of good governance at bay.

However, the publication of telephone or mobile numbers of officers in every office has paid off well because there is an electronic record whether the officer has responded or not. This simple thing will work wonders as everybody uses mobile nowadays. But this should be monitored by the supervisory officer. The Public Grievance Redressal Machinery under the Citizens' Charter in the similar vein is also a fine step towards good governance. I am sure the popular Governments will implement these suggestions because public service is for delivery of service and not for self-aggrandizement.

16-30, June, 2014, Bureaucracy Today

♦♦♦

> *Coming together is a beginning; working together is success.*
>
> **– Henry Ford**

52

Gearing up Govt. Machinery for Better Public Service

The real challenge before the State administrations is how to give the best regulatory services like police service to people, do prompt handling of public grievances and help dispose of pending cases in the revenue and tax bodies and judicial courts and tribunals.

The first and foremost job of the Government is to provide safety and security to people. But the police set-up in India refuses to improve itself whatsoever facilities are provided to it. There is thus a case to infuse outside expertise into the police system, especially into matters not connected with law and order. These include those of recruitment, transfer and posting of police constables, sub-inspectors and higher officers and the prosecution of cases on the pattern of other countries and consistent with the recommendations of various commissions constituted for this purpose, especially the National Police Commission.

Corruption in the police set-up has to be tackled firmly. As the problem is very acute, the change should come from within the police force to keep the image of honest officers intact in the eyes of the public.

The job of time-bound delivery of public services has been provided by many laws but their implementation is very poor. One fails to understand why the supervising superior officers shy away from taking action against defaulters or delinquent government employees.

THE SOLUTION

The solution is to abolish the higher forum of appeal filled up mainly by retired bureaucrats. It is very disheartening to note that the biometric system has been made ineffective by the superior officers by not acting on reports generated by these sophisticated electronic monitoring devices. Similarly, computerization cannot be a panacea for gearing up government machinery unless there is willing co-operation from the higher echelons or higher hierarchies of the bureaucratic structure. The same can be ensured by creating requisite administrative will by political executives who are hard working, transparent and beyond any doubt. Only then the black sheep in government machinery can be isolated and weeded out.

In arbitrary and subjective decisions, especially in revenue and tax matters, the appellate authority should not only be bold to overrule colourable exercise of power by its subordinates but also record its findings that such a decision is vitiated by caprice or personal grudge. Then the arbitrary decision-making and high-handedness by ground level officials will be curtailed and controlled. Though Governments are trying to cut down discretion and delay in decision-making, those officials who do not rectify themselves should be punished.

OBJECTIVE CONSIDERATIONS

It will not be out of place to mention here that the fixing of quarterly targets of doing work and their due monitoring and taking follow up action can do wonders. The appraisal system in government machinery should be based on objective considerations. There should be no interference in the appraisal system.

It was high time government machinery geared itself up as per the demand of time. Otherwise it will be replaced by outsiders like Andhra Pradesh Chief Minister Chandra Babu Naidu who has inducted about 20 MBAs this year as Assistant Collectors to aid and advise the Collectors in their day-to-day functions. Similarly, the Central Government is contemplating inducting about 50 persons from the open market horizontally into the key posts of Joint Secretaries in various Ministries to ensure delivery of due services to citizens.

1–30, September, 2017, Bureaucracy Today

♦♦♦

That government is best which governs the least, because its people discipline themselves.

– Thomas Jefferson

53

People Respond Favourably to Good Governance

Indians have Himalayan patience. They can tolerate the lack of funds and infrastructure and demotivated governmental machinery at work but they cannot agree to corruption, the whimsical work style and partisan working.

After slavery for about 800 years, whosever devoted to their cause they loyally voted for them and made them their rulers for long. This is more perceptible in lower middle classes, including farmers and labourers. For example, Sheikh Abdullah as the Chief Minister of Jammu and Kashmir had fought for the cause of Muslim landless and sharecroppers and distributed substantial quantum of land among them. They venerated him and continued to adore his son and even the grandson. So also is the case with Shrikrishna Sinha of Bihar, the Communist Governments in Kerala, West Bengal and Tripura, Dada Sahab Patil in Maharashtra, Chenna Reddy in Andhra Pradesh, Chowdhary Charan Singh in UP, Gopinath Bordoloi in Assam, Biju Patnaik in Orissa, and Binay Krishna Choudhary in West Bengal.

It was observed that good administration has tackled even terrorism in Jammu and Kashmir and the North Eastern States and Naxalism in Naxalite-infested States. After Ghulam Nabi Azad took over as Chief Minister of J&K, there was a considerable reduction in the number of terrorist attacks and local support to terrorists came down. Similarly after a lot of infusion of Central funds, vocational education and employment to NE boys and girls outside the NE States and control of corruption, separatist agitations and violence have come down. Gogoi as Chief Minister of Assam has successfully tackled separatist violence by his acumenship for development administration and tackling violence with strong hand. In West Bengal, the emergence of Naxalism died down after the administration implemented land reforms like the distribution of Government land in the Naxal-affected areas, constructed roads, schools and hospitals in those areas and tightened the noose on corrupt Panchayat officials.

In Andhra Pradesh, it was due to administrative innovations by the late Chief Minister, SR Reddy, that Naxalism got diluted. He accepted all genuine demands of Naxalites, distributed land to landless persons in the area and at the same time empowered the police force like Greyhounds commandos to tackle the Naxal menace appropriately. In Madhya Pradesh, efforts to give possession to the assignees of Government vested land, i.e., *pattadars,* and the distribution of land records free of cost at the village level, had a salutary effect on anti-Naxal measures. In Chhattisgarh, Chief Minister Raman Singh, known *as Chawl Baba* (rice saint) among the poor people in the Naxal-affected. areas of Bastar and other districts, has won the hearts of the poor tribals and they are gradually coming out of the Naxalite fold. The Central Security forces in the Naxal-affected areas have done a tremendous job of making water and medicines available in villages. In the same way, the Army has done a yeoman's service by exposing Kashmiri boys and girls to other parts of India to generate a feeling among them that they belong to their big family of brothers and sisters in India.

Prime Minister Narendra Modi has done a magic by winning away Muslims and tribals from their traditional base of the Congress by providing them employment in the police force and reaching water and electricity to each and every household even in rural areas. The loyalty is a virtue as per social norms in India. Therefore, if measures of good governance percolate down to the grassroots level, the masses respond positively. They rise against all adverse tendencies and agitations and support the person, political party or the government responsible for providing them with sustainable means of livelihood for many years to come.

16–31, March, 2015, Bureaucracy Today

♦♦♦

No man is good enough to govern another man without that other's consent.

— Abraham Lincoln

54

Cleanliness in Record Room

Prime Minister Narendra Modi has launched the "Clean India" campaign. This is a good beginning to involve people at large in the cleanliness drive. If the visiting members of the public spoil the walls and corners of a government office by spitting pan, gutka or pan bahar around, one cannot really keep the public premises clean.

However, the basic cleanliness drive in a government office has to start from its record room. The record room is a place where old records are preserved or dumped. This room is the nerve centre of an office which at present is the most neglected place. Inefficient or dull personnel are posted to manage the record room.

Unless the record room is cleaned regularly and its old records are sorted out, consigned or destroyed there will be no. further space in the record room. As a result of sorting out, records are consigned to flames. It is a tedious process, without following the due categorization of records. One cannot destroy the old records. The persons managing the record room want more space which is very difficult to get nowadays as it is very cost-effective. After three years, all records except those of permanent nature or of heritage value or of financial nature are to be destroyed. After the lapse of seven years, a person is presumed to be dead in India as per Section 108 of the Indian Evidence Act, 1872. Therefore, there is nothing unusual to destroy records after certain years as per well laid down rules and regulations.

Mr. Anil Kumar Lakhina, IAS, the former Collector and District Magistrate of Ahmednagar, Maharashtra, had practically shown that by cleaning and improving the record room, the efficiency of the Collectorate could be higher.

He emphasized three major reforms.

1. Regulation of the clerk-public contact system,
2. Demystification of the office procedure and the accessibility of documents both to the staff and the public,
3. Better working conditions and the creation of an efficient environment.

As regards first the tables of clerks were cleared of files, registers and papers. Clerks and other senior officials of the section were asked to sit in one hall like in Japan to keep them away from gossiping, leaving their seats and talking to their agents and unnecessary people sitting with them. Clerks were not given any additional chairs in order to curb or curtail unnecessary crowds. Section Officers were provided with glass window's to keep vigil over their subordinates.

On the whole, emphasis was laid on cleanliness, and sanitation. Rooms were whitewashed, floors were carpeted, telephone facilities were provided, wall clocks were put at various places, potable water facilities were provided and toilets were kept clean.

These experiments were further improved upon in 1985 by the then Collector of Sri Ganganagar, Ram Lobhay. Such experiments continued to be done here and there as the idea was very sound. An idea is stronger than the material or monetary resource and lives beyond time and space. Following Lakhina I undertook a cleanliness drive starting from the record room during all my postings for 34 years as an IAS officer.

The Ahmednagar experiment gave a new look to the Collectorate by ensuring more transparency and better preservation of records facilitating their quick retrieval. Nowadays in the post-Lakhina period, it is very easy to keep the record in a few diskettes, floppies, computer drives or hard discs. One has to get old and important records xeroxed scanned and then preserve them in an electronic form. Thus, the record room can be trimmed to a large extent and it can make space available for incoming record documents or files from various sections or wings or tables of an office. It is very important to preserve voluminous land records in the record room.

VERY ROBUST, TIDY OFFICE

As a result, the office looks very robust, tidy and a better place to work where the public will chat or the customer will be entertained in a better way. The old and rusted furniture can be taken out from the record room making way for a new AVTAR' for the new record room in a digital form. Of course, initially there will be a huge cost in xeroxing, scanning and computerizing records but it will save multifold costs by much less maintenance of the record room of the smaller size.

However, it will take many years to replace record rooms by the I. T. record rooms down to the Gram Panchayat level or the Patwari level. In the meantime, the existing record rooms can be free from dump, old and dilapidated records and lizards in sufficient light. A co-operative effort known as "SHRAMDAN" can be undertaken to clean the record room under the leadership of a top officer. However, some work will be required to be done by the PWD or the CPWD which should be no problem.

There are already government guidelines or regulations in vogue on how to maintain the record room like a library but these are followed more in breach. In the Indian Army and the Indian Railways, there is a scientific system of recordkeeping which can be emulated by other government departments.

Thus, proper classification and weeding out the outdated records will provide more space on the tables of clerks to work. This initiative will create lot of additional space in the record room and a more congenial atmosphere of work. In this way, the most neglected place in an office can be the harbinger of efficiency in that office. This will also provide transparent doors between officers and clerks and a well-regulated interaction between the office staff and members of the public.

It is hoped that all offices, whether public or private, will follow the Lakhina experiment of keeping their record rooms more trim but robust, easily accessible and useful for the public or customers by dovetailing with the new information technology. This will be the real obeisance to the Father of the Nation, Mahatma Gandhi by bureaucrats.

16–31, October 2014, Bureaucracy Today

♦♦♦

Verify, the land belongs to him who labours on it.

— Mahatma Gandhi

55

How Can River Cleaning Programmes Become Successful?

River cleaning is a very complex part of civil engineering. It involves civil construction, creating mechanical aeration tanks, installing plants for treating sewage and producing manure and bio-energy, laying interception and diversion sewer lines in congested localities and setting up pumping stations to take sewage out of cities. Technologies are developing everyday to take out sewage beyond rivers. Therefore, experts are required to draft project reports.

LAND ACQUISITION

Land acquisition is a problem due to the non-availability of suitable plots in the dense localities of cities and towns. Even land for laying underground sewer lines is not easily available nor it is there for the construction of pumping stations which are to be located in the city. There will also be the problem of sound pollution due to the operation of pumping stations. However, land can be made available for sewage treatment plants as they have to be invariably located outside the city limits. The way out is to acquire land under the Right to Fair Compensation and Transparency in Land Acquisition, Rehabilitation and Resettlement Act, 2013.

TENDER FLOATING

The floating of tenders in States is generally afflicted with corruption and influence by political executives. The solution is to call and finalize tenders by the National Mission for clean Ganga Authority and after finalizing the tenders they may be handed over to the State authorities or Central public sector undertakings for implementation. This will avert lot of delay in finalizing tenders and placing work orders.

IMPLEMENTATION OF PROJECTS

There should be a mutually agreed time schedule or a bar chart for the implementation of various phases of a project. This should be closely monitored as regards the time schedule and the quality of works. There should be close monitoring by the field officers of the National Mission for Clean Ganga Authority. Or outside monitors may be appointed. The new Namami Ganga Mission does not have field level monitoring agencies or officers which the earlier Ganga Action Plan had in each State who used to visit every city once in a month and suggest steps to overcome problems and delays for each project. They used to have a close liaison with the concerned State Government officer. If the contractor does not mend, his ways, the work may be done departmentally or through a government corporation or public undertaking. It is to be provided that the implementing agency will also maintain the project for three years so that it may execute good work. In the case of a dispute with the contractor, a provision for settling disputes through arbitration or independent third party mediation should invariably be made so that the project is not held up due to a stay by a court of law. The responsibility of officers may be fixed by courts for their arbitrariness or negligence.

OPERATION MANUAL

There should be an operation manual for every plant and the results of its operation should be open to public inspection. Even the quality of effluent water should be publicized in local newspapers every month. After the completion of projects, funds are not available for O&M which defeats the very purpose of projects so important for the well-being of people. Sewer lines should be cleansed properly by local municipal authorities. Thus other concerned departments involved in urban development have to do an equally important job. This also speaks volumes for seeking the co-operation of State Governments in the implementation of river cleaning programmes. If foregoing suggestions are taken into consideration, the river cleaning programmes, including the Namami Ganga Mission, can fulfil the expectations of the people.

1–31, August 2017, Bureaucracy Today

♦♦♦

> *Conservation is a state of harmony between men and land.*
>
> **— Aldo Leopold**

56

The Ganga Cleaning Starts from Home

The Ganga cleaning starts from the home. If solid waste, including plastic, is not allowed to flow into a municipal drain or a sewer line, it will not choke the sewerage system and will not flow into the river Ganga. It can be burnt off as solid waste or recycled. So also if the flesh from tanneries or solid waste from industry is taken out, its effluent treatment plant will work effectively.

As regards municipal sewage in drains or sewer lines, it will be first diverted away from the river through a lifting pumping station which is then fed to a central pumping station. The central pumping station then takes through a rising mains to the sewage treatment plant which has the system of biochemical /biological treatment that separates water from sewage. Water is then used for agricultural purposes and sewage is used as manure. Electric power is also generated through sewage before it is fed to farms as manure.

In the second tier, the arrangement is made to arrest pollution at the source by constructing an electric crematorium, community toilets and individual toilets in houses. Proper arrangement can also be made for the disposal of solid waste by municipal bodies.

The third tier is to prevent pollution from river banks by making pucca river fronts or ghats, planting trees or by releasing biological sources like turtles to eat the dirt or dead bodies. The fourth tier is to create awareness among members of the public by socio-economic units through municipal bodies or NGOs, especially during festivals.

Thus the prerequisite for the city sewage to be diverted is to have a perfect interception and diversion network of sewer lines. If it can be done, the problem of city cleaning is solved to a large extent. The sewerage network is a very costly affair so also the sewage treatment plant. If both these could be achieved, the sewage will not fall into the river which is the main source of river pollution. Now many cheaper technologies are available like pond-holding treatment, sewage treatment through plantation, irrigation through raw sewage and a few foreign technologies like UASB from countries like the Netherlands.

After sewage treatment plants are set up, success depends on the proper operation and maintenance of the system which is generally with municipal bodies or semi-government organisations which lack funds and administrative will to keep the system functioning. There should be bodies having representatives from the public and NGOs to oversee proper operation and maintenance of these costly plants and system so that O & M funds are not misutilized and there should be public notice in newspapers regarding the status of water after treatment at the sewage treatment plant and also the quality of river waters at important points.

DANGEROUS EFFLUENTS

The object is to achieve the BOD in the Ganga or any other river at the level of 3mg/litre or less which is water fit for bathing. However, the effluents from industries are very dangerous as they have many toxic elements like the run-off of chemical fertilizers and insecticides from agricultural fields. Therefore, it has been made mandatory for the polluting industries to set up effluent treatment plants either in their premises or common to the cluster of industries. Even the industries which have ETPs installed, don't operate them sincerely to save the cost on the product in connivance with officials of Pollution Control Boards.

Through partial implementation of the Ganga Action Plan started in 1985, it has been demonstrated that the pollution of river waters can be checked and the pristine glory of the Ganges and other rivers can be restored. Initially there was a mandate of controlling 70% of sewage only falling into the Ganga which had been achieved more or less during the Kumbh 1989 and even during the Mahakumbh at Allahabad in the year 2012 and at Hardwar and Rishikesh and was close to optimum level at Varanasi.

But due to the constant increase of population of the cities in the Ganga basin, the pollution load on river waters also increases because the human population is the greatest polluter. Therefore, it calls for further foolproof measures which require lots of land in cities to place solid waste management facilities, sewage pumps and sewage treatment plants which sometimes become difficult. It is, therefore, better that henceforth sewage treatment plants should be set up with the establishment of new colonies. The decentralization system of planning and action is equally applicable in the technology field. Lastly, by taking up many other rivers for pollution control measures, the attention on the sacred river Ganga has been diluted. It is hoped that all the State Governments, municipal bodies, industries and the public will put up a joint campaign to bring back the purity of river waters, especially that of the Ganga.

♦♦♦

57

Combating Air Pollution in India

The menace of air pollution has surpassed that of water pollution in India. More than eight lakh people die every year due to air pollution in our country apart from causing damage to health. About 3 percent of the GDP is reduced as a result of the ill-effect of air pollution on the Indian economy indirectly.

India has 10 out of the 20 worst cities in the world. The air quality standard internationally recognized is 2. 5 PM whereas in India it is 10 PM. Delhi has a pollution index of 122 PM on an average in a year. During Diwali last year, the air pollution level crossed the danger level beyond 350 PM.

PREVENTIVE MEASURES

There should be proper land use and traffic control plans and an adequate waste disposal arrangement in every town and city of India. Road pavements should be made in concrete to avoid the creation of dust.

Municipal waste should not be burnt but recycled under regulated conditions and not in the open. Even domestic fuel should be gas-based. Municipal bodies should be penalized for their failure to ensure proper disposal of solid waste as per the Supreme Court's order in so many cases.

Though industries are required to install precipitators to prevent the emission of harmful gases as per law, they do not mostly operate these facilities to save costs. Even electric dust collectors should be installed in factories which will add to the output of their workers.

Vehicular pollution has to be tackled primarily at source, that is, cars and trucks should be out of factories only after their compliance with fixed emission norms. Petrol and diesel supplied at outlets should meet pollution control norms which is now being done in India. People should also avoid dependence on private vehicles and should increasingly use mass transport systems like public buses, pooled cars or metro rails wherever these are available. There should be strict enforcement of regulatory measures on vehicles.

Construction is a major source of air pollution. It can be carried on like in foreign countries during night time or after covering the site so that dust particles do not escape here and there. Watering a mining site is also a solution to control pollution.

Spot pollution can be prevented by maintaining cleanliness in homes. The performance of a *Yagna* was considered by *Vedic Rishis* to keep the balance in environment. That is why *Yagna* and self-cleanliness are widely practised, including the use of cow dung to maintain the air and land quality in Indian homes.

The plantation and preservation of trees and forests is another positive way to create better air environment. The plantation of trees by community like the Social Forestry or by individuals or institutions can help create a better air quality.

There is no greater impetus to combat air pollution than creating public awareness. Governments are trying even to switch to clean energy like solar or wind energy and use gas or new environment- friendly technologies in old coal plants. These technologies are now available around the world but these have to be consistent with economic realities and affordability.

Also common people should unite and contribute their bit to make this planet a better place to live in.

April 1-30, 2017, Bureaucracy Today

♦♦♦

It is not living that matters, but living rightly.

— Socrates

58

Preventing Misuse of Social Media

Facebook, Twitter, Whats App and *Google plus* have become common usages. For the time being, the social media has "shown mirage how an isolated person in the present world can remain" connected socially which is an universal urge of people. However, the tremendous popularity of the social media has opened new avenues of commerce as it is the most sought after media to reach the target consumer for all types of business or venture. These companies claim themselves as intermediaries with no responsibility for the contents of the communication.

These social media provide their services free of cost to their users on the Internet. Most of the social media companies like the *Facebook* have their headquarters in the USA but they run their regional headquarters from other countries so as to avoid tax liability under the garb of a double taxation treaty. Thus it has become very difficult to catch them like the flying Internet waves.

This gap was pointed out for the first time through a Public Interest Litigation petition by Virag Gupta, Advocate at the Delhi High Court, in the case, *K N Govindacharya* Vs *Union of India & Ors, WP (C) 3672/2012.* After hearing all parties, the High Court of Delhi passed an epoch-making order on August 23, 2013 that Rule 3 (11) of the Information Technology (Intermediaries Guidelines) Rules, 2011 enjoins upon the intermediary to publish the name of the Grievance Officer on its website and his contact details as well as a mechanism by which users or any victim who suffers as a result of access or usage of computer resource can approach him. The Grievance Officer shall redress the complaint within one month from the date of receipt of the complaint. But most of these companies don't have their Grievance Officers in India which creates a problem for Internet users and the public which became evident during the Uber App Taxi Service episode in which a cab passenger was raped by the cab driver. Thus, the social media must have their Grievance Officers in India so as to locate them physically in case of emergent situation.

Following the directions of the Delhi High Court in the case, the Government of India through the Department of Electronics and IT advised its employees, inter alia under the Public Records Act, 1993 that while employees are using the social media in their personal capacity,

- they must clearly identify themselves,
- confidential information must not be divulged,
- their views should not be seen to represent the official view unless authorized to do so,
- for any official work involving transmission of public records, they must use an Email identity connected to a server, located in India and for this purpose they may preferably take the service of the National Information Centre (NIC).

Section 4 of the Public Records Act prohibits taking of public records out of India.

Regarding email communications, the Department of Electronics and IT, Government of India, advised further in its circular dated 27.11. 2014 (No. 2 (103)/2014 - CERT, "It has been observed that a number' of officials in the Ministries/ Departments in the Central and State Governments are using private mail services, particularly hosted and operated from outside India, for official communications. Such official communications are government and also public records. It is to mention that data pertaining to such emails and web services is stored by these service providers outside India and is fully under their control. At the time of any security breach, incident on data loss it becomes very difficult to obtain data from these service providers apart from the possibility of leakage of information as they are controlled by the service providers outside the country."

Thus, all that glitters is not gold as regards social media also. Excessive use of social media has caused isolation and depression among its users in their personal life.

♦♦♦

> *Atmano Deepo Bhav (Be like a lamp; be a light unto thyself).*
>
> — ***Gautam Buddha***

59

Better to Continue Present Constitutional Status of Delhi-NCT

At the time of Independence, Delhi was allowed to be governed through the Chief Commissioner under the overall control of the Government of India. After the States Reorganisation Act, 1956, Delhi was converted into a Union Territory and the Chief Commissioner was replaced by the Lieutenant Governor. However, more powers were decentralized by the 69th Amendment of the Constitution in 1991 when the UT of Delhi was conferred a status of NCT of Delhi having its own elected Legislative Assembly like Puducherry. But the Legislative Assembly of Delhi was not to have any power with respect to public order, police and land contained in the State List of Second Schedule of the Constitution. Thus, the NCT of Delhi has been conferred only limited autonomy keeping the basic framework of the Constitution in mind to preserve the strong Centre. The President has been given further dominant powers in all matters, where there will be difference of opinion between Ministers and the Lieutenant Governor (Art 239 AA(4) Provision) whereas in States the Governor is bound to act on the aid and advice of the Council of Ministers.

According to constitutional expert Ivor Jennings, India is a federation with strong centralized tendencies. In a practical situation, the Central Government at Delhi will not be able to function with peace and free mind if its Ministers, officers and staff are constantly scared of the local Government of Delhi on the score of vigilance or law and order. The present AAP

(Aam Adami Party) Government with a brute majority in the Assembly is an agitational government like the erstwhile Left Front Governments in West Bengal and Kerala. In such a situation, the Central Government will not be able to take bold and fast decisions unless the subjects of police and public order are with it. However, the Central Government, while having control of the Police force in Delhi should have an independent Minister of State for Delhi in the Ministry of Home Affairs. It is observed that a Joint Secretary in charge of UTs is occupied with hundred other things and cannot devote fully nor has the calibre to handle the police in the National Capital Territory of Delhi.

We have observed palpable violations of diplomatic privileges by the local government or State Government in a federal structure in the World which affected foreign relations and there by national interests because the local Government is not expert in that field. An example is the Devyani Khobragade, an Indian diplomat's case in USA. There are many such instances. That is one reason why Vatican City has been given an independent status of a country so that the Pope is free from the clutches of the local Government or its enforcement agencies and can even pass strictures for violation of the code of Christianity against the country of his domicile.

The Transaction of Business Rules which emanate from the Constitution and Law provide that the Lieutenant Governor has to keep the President informed beforehand about the appointment of Chief Secretary, Police Commissioner, Secretary (Home) and Secretary (Land), matters affecting the interests of minorities, Scheduled Castes and backward classes and important matters affecting the peace and order of the NCT of Delhi. On the other hand, the Delhi- NCT administration has to ensure as a representative of governance of the Union of India that people from all States and regions are not discriminated against.

Thus, the Delhi-NCT is basically a city State which was not made even 'C' category State after due consideration. The Sarkaria-Balakrishnan Committee also opposed a separate State status for Delhi. Within the present framework, the Government of Delhi-NCT has lot of subjects and works relating to public welfare and city management.

More autonomy and decentralization of power are well accepted principles of good governance but these are to be based on history past practices and experiences. In the present scenario, where States are not able to manage their finances, maintain law and order and discipline their public servants, it is better that the present constitutional status of Delhi-NCT continues.

16–31 July, 2015, Bureaucracy Today

◆◆◆

The journey of a thousand miles begins with one step.

— Lao Tzu

60

Skilling India is a Very Tough Job

The Skill Development Scheme of the Indian Government aims at introducing approved training programmes. The National Skill Development Corporation is the implementing agency for this Scheme. Though 10 lakh youths are to be trained under the Scheme in one year, it is yet to percolate down to the grassroots level.

There should be a committee headed by the Chairman of a Zilla Parishad or the District Magistrate which can identify the requirements of jobs, at the district or nearby areas and arrange for giving training firstly in district and then in the fields outside the State or the country. It is good that the task is now being assigned to private agencies because the programme of placing candidates for internships in Government bodies during the previous years has failed. Polytechnics and Industrial Training Institutes did not update their courses nor did they introduce new training streams like those for the repair of mobiles, cars and motorcycles and for driving, cooking, nursing, cleaning, guarding, gardening, baby care, physiotherapy, beauty saloon, yoga, making medicines at home, plastic industry and printing by hand.

At present, the institutes, under the Scheme are sending newly trained candidates to distant centres of large employment in various fields like those in Coimbatore, Kolkata, Mumbai, Bengaluru, Delhi and Gujarat. Many of them will come back after sometime due to inadequate savings and local resistance.

There is a need to devise courses or training streams according to the availability of local jobs. However, as employment of Indians is spreading all over the world, there should be some Government or semi-government agency which will place these trained people around the world, will guarantee their good conduct in foreign countries and will also insure the employees against risks or hazards.

Skilling is also required for the IT sector where the Government can open centres to train IT boys and girls in improving their English language through learning grammar. There is an arrangement to teach languages in IITs in India which requires to be introduced in other engineering colleges. Otherwise a large number of technical graduates will be frustrated for not finding jobs.

At the international level, India has to search for new avenues for large-scale employment. These fields can be audit and accounts and law in which the highly skilled boys and girls from India can find jobs abroad.

Now the problem remains how India, can compete with other countries like Bangladesh and China which produce cheap garments and toys, respectively. Here our small and cottage industries sector can be of great help. Farmers sit idle for more than five months in a year. They have great talent to work artistically through their hands. Unfortunately, the Government has withdrawn a network of Krishi Sahayak or farmers' friends. They should again be deployed in a modified form. These old institutions should be given time to update themselves - Still an ordinary Indian farmer has not become internet-savvy. The next generation will pick up Mobile and Internet technology properly.

In conclusion, we can say that the Skill Development Scheme should cover all fields, especially evergreen Indian sectors. There should be equal emphasis on innovation and improvement in our fields of strength like IT, garment making and farming and allied agriculture. There should be constant monitoring so that trainees do not run away with stipends without due learning.

♦♦♦

61

Improving CSR Initiatives

Works under the Corporate Social Responsibility obligation of companies have generated lot of enthusiasm and respect towards the corporate world which was perceived so far as a profit making machine. The companies have also come forward in social regeneration by undertaking projects like the conservation of tigers in the Sunderbans, West Bengal, training drivers in accident-free driving, popularizing mobile technology in the health, education, agriculture and environment sectors, sponsoring girl children for education, helping physically challenged persons, adopting villages, constructing toilet blocks in schools and a host of other activities.

This latest move has certainly made social and charitable activities of Indian companies in a systematic and professional manner which was earlier based on the whims and fancies of promoters, Directors, the Chairman or Managing Director of a big company or a group of companies. In fact, many temples, schools, hospitals and *dharamshalas* in the country have come up out of such funds which remained unnamed till the new statutory provision "CSR" was coined by the new Companies Act, 2013 (Section 135). Under the new stipulation, only those companies are covered which have a net worth of ₹ 500 crore or more each or turnover of ₹ 1,000 crore or more or a net profit of ₹ 5 crore or more during a financial year.

Lot of autonomy is provided to companies to undertake CSR activities. It is better if the companies are allowed to take up welfare activities in the vicinity where their manufacturing units are located so that they may win the support of local populace. It is essential to have local support to run a company smoothly. The TISCO company has not seen a strike because it undertook lot of social welfare activities in Tatanagar and in nearby tribal villages. By and large municipal services are run by the TISCO and they have made Tatanagar an ideal city. The Birlas have also set up many of their townships adjoining their plants which have paid them dividends in running plants smoothly with local allegiance.

Of course, now this is becoming a costly affair, especially with the dwindling profits of those old units. But the concept still holds good. Secondly, Indian corporates should be allowed to invest in research in line with their products. Indian manufacturing is suffering largely because of inadequate research and development work.

Such contribution can be provided to technology incubators located within academic institutions like IITs and universities and to implement research findings on the field without any delay which is not available in public domain.

If the *Make in India* campaign is to be made successful and vibrant, this initiative is a must. Otherwise indigenous companies will not be able to stand in competition against foreign companies and multinationals (MNCs) and the MNCs- and TMNCs will continue to expropriate India's resources and wealth. As on date, foreign companies are lagging behind in CSR initiatives.

This will also give a push to unattended areas of manufacturing in view of the new developments and innovations. As a result, additional wealth will be generated and the corporate world in India will be able to contribute more for . welfare activities for the rural and urban poor.

Companies should be allowed autonomy to use such funds. At the initial stage, it will, not be advisable to have contributions by companies through notifications by the Central Government for the "Swachh Bharat Kosh" or the "Clean Ganga Fund". Of course, the companies should be given an option and autonomy to be a partner or a contributor in a Government project or programme. The September, 2015 report by the high-level committee chaired by Anil Baijal on improved monitoring of the implementation of Corporate Social Responsibility policy also recommends autonomy for companies in CSR.

1–15, March 2016, Bureaucracy Today

♦♦♦

> *If India is not to perish, we here to begin with lower rung of ladder.......My conception of 'Swaraj' is not concentration of authority in a few but the acquisition of the capacity in many to regulate authority.*
>
> **— M.K. Gandhi**

62

Small is Beautiful

British economist EF Schumacher propounded a famous theory, *'Small is Beautiful'*, way back in the year 1975 which is still relevant and can be *inter alia* applied in the social, political and administrative fields. This quote is the classic of common sense economics upon which trends in our society are noticed. This speaks of a decentralized system and appropriate technology with human face in all areas and is opposed to monopolization and centralization. According to Schumacher, truths are fundamentally stable regardless of time, culture or the prevailing economic system. Human activity can surpass production by the machine or the State.

This has been amply demonstrated during the Chennai flood in the year 2016 where hundreds of lives of animals and human-beings were saved by a few local spirited persons without any affiliation with any group or organization and produced output better than State apparatus. Similarly, disaster can be tackled only by the local people immediately. For example, in case of any serious train or air accident, it is the local people who come and rescue the injured persons before help is rushed from the administration. Thus the village level or municipal level local self-governments or local councils are the real organizations; which can deliver results during emergencies and normal times.

Modern economic theories have resulted in disastrous environment and adverse social consequences. Therefore, it is high time that there should be a good mix of the grassroots level approach and the high production approach.

The same theory holds good in the fields of administration and management of grassroots level institutions. In modern administration or management, middle level and lower level workers or employees are feeling overlooked by the top management. That is one of the reasons why workers are feeling alienated and indifferent at their workplace and are not able to deliver their best which is impeding the progress of the organization, society and the country. The delegation of roles is essential to run all organizations, especially large organizations like the Government. The public doesn't have the reach to the top man in the bureaucracy. Members of the public come into contact with lower level officials and form opinion about the Government on the basis of response from lower level officials. If a lower level functionary is delegated a job, his accountability can be properly fixed. But in India, people have feudal mentality. They want to stick to the power and do not want to delegate their power or authority.

In a political party, only the president exercises all powers and is always in public limelight. Even a Cabinet Minister would not like to part with his powers or delegate his work to his junior Minister. This creates overburdening of the senior Minister and taking decisions is delayed and the quality of decisions suffers. In the private sector, the owner doesn't want to delegate his authority because most of the industries in India are family-owned. As a result, Indian industries have done badly in competition with multinationals. Now the familial organizations are giving way to professional organizations which is the only way out to survive and progress in the present global environment. However, in India, there is good distribution or delegation of powers among bureaucrats formally. But the top man holds the power of decision-making and sometimes keeps key powers with him, including the procedural ones because sometime procedural issues involve more important political and financial implications. This is bad. The wielding of essential power is good but others should be allowed to contribute their best. Then only the organization can keep pace and progress in the age of globalization, Internet and Information Technology.

1–15, 2016, January, Bureaucracy Today

♦♦♦

63

Taking District Administration to Doorstep of Citizens

The district administration is the axis of the Indian administration. However, of late there have been several instances of the district system headed by the Collector becoming indifferent and opaque to people's grievances. Though many of its developmental duties have been delegated to panchayat bodies, most of the regulatory activities like fixing land revenue, checking the commission of petty crimes, resolving minor civil disputes and food and supplies matters, the regulation of motor vehicles, handling emergency issues relating to floods and drought and holding elections are still with the district administration. There are many innovative ways in practice in different Indian States through which people's grievances are being sorted out. One such practice is in vogue in Uttar Pradesh under which "Tehsil Divas" and "Thana Divas" are observed on fixed days at least twice in a month.

Petitions of public grievances are invited on the prescribed performa or online for their resolution on "Tehsil Divas" or "Thana Divas" on the first and third Tuesday of every month. Then notices are sent to the opposite parties.

If the parties agree to settle the issue or do not object on valid grounds to the resolution of a dispute, then such cases are listed on the first and third Saturday of every month as "Samadhan Day".

All parties, including the concerned government officials, are requested to be present at the Tehsil or police station concerned for an amicable settlement of the dispute. On the appointed day, everybody, including senior officers like the SDO and the District Magistrate, turns up at the Tehsil. In the presence of senior officers, the matter is deliberated threadbare with all its legal aspects.

If there is some spot inquiry report by a field level official or an inspector that is placed for consideration. After that a settlement is placed. If the one side doesn't accept the settlement, the concerned revenue or police officer is asked to do the needful to enforce the decision at the site like giving the possession of land in question, the demarcation of the disputed piece of land, taking the possession of government or panchayat land or the right of way, making a correction in the record of land reinstatement or allowing a share to the share-cropper, the settlement of a dispute regarding an irrigation channel, or a pond or a canal and registering an FIR by the police.

Even matters like the settlement of a family dispute or a marriage dispute or a petty criminal dispute concerning the theft of a crop or cattle, the settlement of a dispute regarding the payment of wages by a contractor or under a government scheme like the MGNREGA scheme, the non-receipt of government payments by contractors or the old age pension or the sanction of a bank loan or subsidy, the demand for a bribe by a government official, the non-receipt of a Scheduled Caste or a Scheduled Tribe or a domicile certificate or government scholarship and the demand for high fees by Government doctors or by private hospitals are considered.

About 1.8 crore applications are shown disposed of by the UP Government through such a mechanism where Benaras Division is on the top whereas Lucknow district is the last.

The forum acts as a Gram Nyayalaya in the absence of such an institute at the block level. No advocate is required to be present on behalf of any party.

DISADVANTAGE

The main disadvantage of this system is that when the settlement goes for enforcement by the department concerned, its officials analyse all pros and cons in the file and take usual time in disposing of the dispute.

The efficacy of the system is, however, gradually declining.

1–15, January, 2017, Bureaucracy Today

♦♦♦

Government of the people, by the people, for the people, shall not perish from the Earth

– Abraham Lincoln

64

Indians should Utilize Weekends More Fruitfully

As per official statistics, a Mexican worker works for 2,228 hours in a year, a South Korea worker, spends 2,013 hours at workplace followed by those of Malta, and Ireland. The United States has been pushed back to the 17th position because of 1,789 hours of work by its industrial worker. In Israel, a worker spends 1,853 hours on an average. It was high time India reviewed its working hours system, especially in view of its optimistic *Make in India* programme.

As per the Factories Act 1948, an adult industrial worker in India is required to work at least for 48 hours in a week. He is, however, not allowed to work in a factory for more than nine hours' in a day with half-an-hour for rest. Thus, the average working hours for six days for a worker in India come to 5.6 or six hours a day excluding a half-an-hour lunch break. The situation is worse in offices with white collar jobs. The staff and officers indulge in lot of gossiping during office hours. Lower level functionaries hardly devote time to analyse the pros and cons of the issues before them. As a result, the quantum of output as well as the quality of work suffers.

If India has to make its place in the comity of developed nations, the working hours should not be less than eight hours a day. In North Korea under a dictator, a worker works for 16 hours in a labour camp. The situation of a labour hostel in China is not very different but people there work voluntarily to put China on top of the world. In China, the working duration is from 8 am to 5 pm or from 9 am to 6 pm. Even the Western countries are ahead of India in having total working hours. India can compensate by reducing the number of holidays and utilizing weekends. The number of holidays in India is perhaps the highest in the World and is constantly rising from its present level at 16 due to pressure from various quarters. The US has 10 days as holiday in a year whereas the UK has eight holidays in a year.

In the Western world, weekends are utilized in frolicking on tourist spots, beaches, or in hotels or motels. As a result, the enjoyment during weekends brings more psychological or mental burden rather than a flow of energy to work. The Indians have a great culture. They utilize weekends to meet their parents, visit temples, mosques or churches or attend moral discourses, do yoga, *pranayama* or meditation, or spend time in leisure, study or writing. Many great works of science, music, paintings and literature have been produced during the leisure hours. This equips people with lot of positive energy which will unfold during the next week. As a result, the Indians will provide a better output. Nowadays, many white and blue collar workers in India, apart from doing their domestic chores and meeting their family obligations, engage themselves in social service at charitable organizations, teaching the poor and needy children and students or helping the have-nots in society. Many join 'Shramdan" to clean their surroundings or public places.

It is surprising that there is an increasing trend in our country to welcome holidays. It is becoming an infection. India is a land of *'karma'* or work. According to the *Bhagwad Gita,* if a person does not do positive action, there will be a negative action on him. Work generates good qualities in a human being. Let us, therefore, welcome different types of *'karma'* which we miss during the usual course of work to get fulfilment. This can not only enrich one's personality and psychology but can also release immense energy during work which will put India on the road to progress and prosperity.

1–15, May, 2016, Bureaucracy Today

♦♦♦

65

Privatization is not the Panacea

The concept of privatization means bringing more discipline in market forces mainly through competition. The privatization system was introduced in the UK in 1979 by the Thatcher, Government which sent its waves to other countries.

The Indian Government initiated structural reforms in 1991 with an obligation of making the economy more efficient and competitive and saving it from a slide into the doom.

Since then India has been making forays into privatization but with caution. One midway solution of public-private partnership is now an accepted instrument. But PPP projects did not come out with expected success due to the usual phenomenon of withholding investment of funds by the partner, the slow decision making process followed by Government functionaries because of their ulterior motives, a long gestation period for projects and political hovering around after private players started making profit. One has not to forget the fundamental proposition that private players come into the public domain to make profit and not for charity.

The ailing public sector enterprises of the Central Government are being made efficient and competitive through the Department of Disinvestment. It promotes people's ownership of Central public sector enterprises through disinvestment, releases resources for capital investment, makes improvement in corporate governance through the listing of CPSEs (Central Public Sector Enterprises) on the stock exchange and greater transparency and accountability in PSUs. They offer equity for sale or private infusion of equity into CPSEs and the appointment of advisors, independent company directors and outside arbitrators. The proceeds of disinvestment were channelized into the drastically needed National Investment Fund. This has brought down the annual budget investment in CPSEs considerably which can be used for the benefit of rural and urban poor people.

But the success has not been achieved at the expected leveL The higher authorities of Central PSEs and State PSUs still complain of governmental control through the appointment of CEOs and the introduction of a vigilance mechanism.

In fact, with the structural charges, the mindset of those running the public sector in India has not changed. They are still slow in decision-making. The management still fears to take disciplinary action against employees. There is red-tapism in the public sector. And the ghost of corruption still haunts the public sector in India.

The more efficient and cheaper products from multinational companies and China are not allowing the public sector to monopolize the market in India. As a result, the level of profits of *Navratna* PSU companies like SAIL and BHEL is gradually shrinking. They have to find out new markets in Africa and Latin America apart from introducing product transformations.

The IT giants of India are suffering from the same malaise. To be more competitive they require an intensely qualified and sincere workforce in the field. However, the airlines and the telecom industry in India are among the good performers.

The favourite project of Digital India will provide more relief. But the real solution lies elsewhere. Political executives have to do more administration than politics. Bureaucrats should enforce due accountability and transparency in the system even at the cost of removing or dismissing many government employees. The management of public sector units has to be more innovative and speedy to keep pace with developments elsewhere in the developed countries. There should be a perfect regulatory mechanism in place.

The Competition Commission of India and the Telecom Regulatory Authority are doing a good job by punishing car and mobile companies which are trying to exploit consumers by providing repair and maintenance services at a very high cost so also in the fields of medicine, education and real estate. It is hoped that the regulatory mechanism authorities in India will come up to the mark to earn the blessings of the Indian people.

16–29, February, 2016, Bureaucracy Today

♦♦♦

> *If a free society cannot help the many who are poor, it cannot save the few who are rich.*
>
> **— John F. Kennedy**

66

Corruption also in Private Sector: How can it be Controlled?

Corruption in the private sector has assumed such gigantic proportions that business or industry or service organizations will collapse under its weight unless some emergent steps are taken to control it.

In the private sector, bribe is reportedly given to take undue advantage of competition with other industries or business because of changes in Government policies or regulations, or decisions.

Secondly, a private company or an enterprise pays bribe if it is caught in a tax evasion case or in a serious irregularity in its business operations. In such contingencies, Government tax officers exploit the fear of private company officials being punished. If the proprietor, director or partner of a private enterprise is well aware of Government rules and regulations, he will not come under pressure. After all in Government or semi-Government transactions, there is a provision of appeal against every adverse decision. The person against whom an adverse action is proposed to be taken will invariably be given an opportunity of getting a hearing and he can put up his case without undue pressure or fear.

Thus the lack of knowledge of Government rules or hard work is a cause of corruption in the private sector whose officials do not exert much to go deep into complex issues and suggest the easiest way to their bosses to get things done by bribing Government officials. If the top management rejects their suggestions, they will have to find out legal ways and means to solve a problem. The old bosses easily agree with their officials as they have the experience of the times when people were not so much conscious and public servants were top deciding authorities in the system. Nowadays, public servants are not the undisputed masters. There are more knowledgeable persons in the private sector who can get the work done either with the help of new technology or IT innovations or with the help of the Right To Information Act or the Service Delivery Act in force.

The private sector takes everything as a challenge and its officials find a management solution for every problem. It is, therefore, suggested that there should be a "corruption management team" in every middle and large private sector organization that can study the problem, analyse its pro and cons and suggest legal solutions or the last grievance channel for the problem. Members of such a team will have to be expert in knowing Government procedures, rules and connected laws and also have to be aware of the hierarchy of Government officers involved in the transaction. Earlier Government machinery was an opaque organization. Nowadays, most of the information is on the website of "the department or the Ministry concerned though phone numbers may not be communicative. But one can find most of the latest rules or procedures on the Government website which can be further researched to arrive at a solution. However, one still fails to understand how commercial disputes can be solved expeditiously because there is a large pendency of cases in courts. It can still be debated whether the "corruption management team" in the private sector should also handle court cases.

Supervision and control on corruption internally and externally in the private sector is now a legal requirement as India has ratified the United Nations Convention on Corruption and the process of amending the Prevention of Corruption Act, 1988 is at an advanced stage making the bribe giver criminally liable and abettor punishable with up to five years' jail and not less than six months' imprisonment and also liable to pay fine. This charge can also be framed against the top private management as it is the ultimate beneficiary as it happened in the recent coal mine allocation case involving a Madhya Pradesh-based company.

1-31, July, 2017, Bureaucracy Today

♦♦♦

Economy is the art of making the most of life.

– George Bernard Shaw

67

Black Money Holders 'Running Parallel Economy' in India

The pernicious problem of black money in India has been affecting the vitals of the Indian economy for a long time. It is good for the nation that the Modi Government has become highly active in getting the grip of the problem. It has got the Black Money Act, 2015 passed by Parliament. Experts opine that there is a parallel economy in India allegedly being run by holders of black money. It is known as unaccounted or illegal money. It is increasing the inequalities in income and wealth. This new breed of black rich cause many illegal and unproductive activities in society.

Many estimates of black money have been in circulation in India. According to one estimate, about 23 to 26 per cent of the Gross Domestic Product of India is the below average of about 38.7 percent among developing countries. An estimate says that the black money in circulation is from ₹ 10 lakh crore to ₹ 15 lakh crore. This will amount to about ₹ 10,000 per Indian citizen.

However, the estimates by the Wanchoo Committee, Rangneker, Chopra, NIPFP and Guptas did not cross ₹ 1,49,297 crore up to 1987-88. What is not understood how there is a sudden surge in various figures of black money which may not be based on facts. According to the White Paper report on Black Money in India, published in May 2012 by the Government of India, the total amounts deposited in all Swiss banks, at the end of 2010 by citizens of India were ₹ 92.95 billion *i.e.* ₹ 6,04,175 crore. In 2011, the Government of India received the names of 782 Indians who had accounts with the HSBC Bank. The amount is about 700 folds less than what was alleged in some media reports.

According to the MC Joshi Committee report submitted in January 2012, two major political parties in India spent about ₹ 25,000 crore in a year. The real estate sector of the Indian economy which accounts for 11 percent of India's GDP is the major absorbent of black money. A large number of transactions in real estate are not reported and are beyond reach because of the complicated land issues involved. Other sectors of the Indian economy include equity trading market, mining permits, bullion, non-profit organizations, illegal rackets of hawala and ostentatious expenditure in personal life.

Whenever there is pressure on black money, it goes down in the dens or caves. And its adverse effect is seen on the economy, especially in the real estate sector when its activities become slack. The life style market is another casualty and the withdrawal of funds from the stock exchange results in further devaluation of the rupee.

Suggestions are being given to check the generation of black money by reducing excessive income tax income rates, reporting global financial transactions above a threshold limit in line with the USA Patriot Act and demonetizing currency notes of high values as suggested by Baba Ramdev.

In India there is a vast machinery of the Income Tax Department for International Taxation exclusively. It is spread over 510 cities and towns in 800 buildings having 55,000 officers and employees along with police personnel. But the government machinery has not done its job properly. It is, therefore, advisable that more attention should be given to preventing further generation or hoarding of black money rather than pursuing the offenders which is disproportionate to the amount spent to collect evidence against them.

16–30, November, 2015, Bureaucracy Today

♦♦♦

Black incomes are accentuating the inequalities in income and wealth and breeding a new class of 'black' rich in a society which is already harshly stratified.

– D.K. Rangnekar

68

Black Money: How Black it is?

There is a parallel economy in India allegedly being run by holders of black money. It is known as unaccounted or illegal money. It is increasing the inequalities in income and wealth. This new breed of black rich create imbalance in the economy and cause many illegal and unproductive activities in society.

There are many estimates of black money in circulation at different points of time. It is estimated at about 23 to 26 per cent of the Gross Domestic Product of India which is below average of about 38.7 percent among developing countries. But according to a modest estimate, the black money in circulation is from ₹ 10 lakh crore to ₹ 15 lakh crore, which will amount to ₹ 10, 000 approximately per Indian citizen.

However, the estimates by the Wanchoo Committee, Rangneker, Chopra, NIPFP and Guptas did not cross ₹ 1,49,297 crore up to 1987-88. What is not understood how there is a sudden surge in various figures of black money which may not be based on facts. According to the White Paper report on Black Money in India, published in May 2012 by the Government of India, the total amounts deposited in all Swiss banks, at the end of 2010 by citizens of India were ₹ 92.95 billion *i.e.* ₹ 6,04,175 crore. In 2011, the Government of India received the names of 782 Indians who had accounts with the HSBC. The amount is about 700 fold less than what was alleged in some media reports.

According to the MC Joshi Committee report submitted in January 2012, during the General Election, two major political parties in India spent about ₹ 25,000 crore in a year. The real estate sector of the Indian economy which accounts for 11 percent of India's GDP is the major absorbent of black money. A large number of transactions in real estate are not reported and are beyond reach because of the complicated land issues involved. Other sectors of the Indian economy include equity trading market, mining permits, bullion, non-profit organizations, illegal rackets of hawala and ostentatious expenditure in personal life.

Whenever there is pressure on black money, it goes down in the dens or caves. And its adverse effect is seen on the economy, especially in the real estate sector when its activities become stack. The life style market is another casualty and the withdrawal of funds from the stock exchange results in further devaluation of the rupee.

Suggestions are being given to check the generation of black money by reducing excessive income tax rates, announcing a voluntary disclosure scheme, reporting global financial transactions above a threshold limit in line with the USA Patriot Act and demonetizing currency notes of high values of ₹ 500 and ₹ 1000 as suggested by Baba Ramdev.

In India there is a vast machinery of the Income Tax Department for International Taxation exclusively. It is spread over 510 cities and towns in 800 buildings having 55,000 officers and employees along with police personnel. But the government machinery has not done its job properly. It is, therefore, advisable that more attention should be given to preventing further generation or hoarding of black money rather than pursuing the offenders disproportionate to the amount spent to collect evidence against them.

16–31, October, 2015, Bureaucracy Today

♦♦♦

69

How Tax Havens Function

There is a great debate going on in India as to how the inflow of black money can be controlled from tax havens. The tax havens are generally small countries which do not have a sustainable gross domestic product. But as sovereign States they can give lot of concessions in all types of taxes just to encourage economic activity in their jurisdictions. These economic or financial transactions themselves can create a large number of white-collar jobs in these countries as a result of which they will not have to look for other avenues for their people.

These activities get a fillip when these countries have liberal bilateral tax treaties or understanding with India. Then there is no apprehension to go in for transactions through these countries.

Mauritius is one such example which has favourable tax treaties with India and a few small countries in Europe. These countries are advanced due to the activities of allegedly illegal foreign funds there.

Multinational or transmultinational companies open their units in these tax havens so that their subsidiaries may function without any additional liability of tax in tax haven countries taking advantage of the existing legal and tax framework of India. Then they route their investments through these companies to those countries with whom these countries have treaties to avoid double taxation. There are some shell or fake companies or incorporates registered in these tax havens without the verification of their whereabouts or permanent offices or the veracity of authorized agents or directors signing on behalf of these companies formed and registered there. If subsequently these companies are hauled up for indulging in dubious deals in other countries, none will be physically available to fix accountability. There are a number of such companies without actual existence on the ground in Mauritius. There are some laws in Mauritius but they are not very effective.

These companies reportedly only make bank transactions through Mauritius banks. The banks there are not concerned whether the money is black or white. Now Indian banks like the SBI and the BoB have also opened up their units in Mauritius which will facilitate tax avoiding transactions. These companies, it is said, ply back the profits to their actual masters. No action could probably be taken by tax haven countries because they don't have a requisite administrative framework nor the political or administrative will as these companies bring economic activity in those countries.

It is not easy to terminate the treaty since the other country will not accept the evidence of malpractices placed by India like Pakistan which never accepts that there are terrorists in that country though it is visible fact as sunlight during the day.

HISTORICAL AND CULTURAL TIES

Secondly, India has historical and cultural ties with countries like Mauritius as another small India in the Indian Ocean. Therefore the Indian psyche would not like to break economic ties with a country like Mauritius because economic ties in the present international scenario do affect bilateral relations. India requires the support of these sovereign countries to focus its voice before the international community like the U.N. at least as a leader of the developing countries.

Thirdly, Foreign Direct Investment is very much sought after. It is the only way to progress from the status of a developing country to a developed nation.

Chanakya, the great economist of ancient India, has suggested a wayout. According to him, an informant who supplies information about embezzlement under preparation should get one-sixth of the amount in question as an award. If he happens to be a government servant, he should get one-twelfth of the amount. Chanakya says that a government servant is like a fish which knows what is happening under water.

Therefore, utmost vigilance is needed on overt transactions in India like investments in the real estate sector and equity under the Prevention of Money Laundering Act, 2002.

Some good steps have already been taken by the Indian Government to check black money and some more will be appreciated by the public at large.

1–15, December, 2015, Bureaucracy Today

♦♦♦

> *We are suffering just now from a bad attack of economic pessimism.*
>
> **— J.M. Keynes**

70

Positive Approach to Demonetisation

No purpose will be served by debating whether the recent demonetisation of high value currency notes was right or wrong. India has already gone through the process of demonetisation. Let us discuss how we can derive maximum gain from this economic reform.

It has been revealed that India doesn't have that big amount of black money *i.e.* 30% of the economy that was so far estimated. Now the critics of black money say that it is mostly parked in the real estate or the housing sector. It will be very difficult to detect and catch the black money converted into housing property in spite of the enactment of the new Benami Transactions (Prohibition) Amendment Act, 2016 as was the fate of the earlier Benami Transactions (Prohibition) Act, 1988 due to procedural deficiencies.

Hardly few properties could be brought to public use under the earlier Act. It speaks a lot about the machinery and process involved to unearth benami properties. Though the new Act is a considerable improvement over the earlier Act, it will have to overcome the uphill task in spite of strong political will. The recent process of demonetisation has proved that bankers cannot be relied upon to take up such a big challenge.

Similarly, the Income tax Department, the Enforcement Directorate and the CBI are not equipped with staff to undertake investigation in a huge number of cases in which many will not yield positive results.

The way out is to adopt more and more innovative settlement and disclosure schemes like the Voluntary Disclosure Scheme. Black money holders would like to come out in the public domain to do charitable work under definite projects. They may be allowed to register under the Societies Registration Act, 1860 and may seek exemption under Sections 11 and 80G of the Indian Income Tax Act, 1961. However, there should be effective control of the local administration over such trusts so much so that District Collectors should be made their ex-officio Chairmen.

'CASHLESS TRANSACTIONS'

The second solution given is that of "cashless transactions". It is a welcome move but it will take lot of time to reach the grassroots level in spite of making it Internet-free on *Bhim App* because of computer illiteracy in rural areas. However, the cashless economy will have a push once people are assured that they will not be cheated by a new mushroom growth of cashless Internet companies on the pattern of many ponzi companies in the past. These new-born cashless transaction companies don't have their pre-defined offices in India and the Uber and Ola taxi companies, Facebook, WhatsApp, Twitter, Google and other digital companies have their offices and main servers in the USA, Ireland or in Singapore. Such companies should be duly registered in India and their CEOs and Directors should be available physically in India to redress the grievances of customers or users. Otherwise even after lifting the veil of the company under the new Benami Transactions (Prohibition) Act, 2016, the Director will not be amenable to Indian laws or courts.

However, governmental efforts are praiseworthy. But the Central Government should set up one division in the Ministry of Finance with the experts of the Ministry of Electronics and the Ministry of Consumer Affairs. This division should centrally monitor these cashless transaction companies so that a bona fide person using the cashless mechanism is not defrauded. That division should also monitor the cashless mechanism adopted even by all banks, including government ones and persons responsible in each of such companies should be in the public domain to bring more transparency and accountability in cashless transactions.

It is a fact that cashless transactions will help fight corruption and reduce overhead expenditure, including *Inspector Raj* but this has to be adopted with due safeguards of law and technology.

16–31, January, 2017, Bureaucracy Today

♦♦♦

Democratic governments, by their nature, are pressure-responders rather than problem anticipators.

— Walter W. Heller

71

Should Death Penalty be Abolished in India?

Whenever there is any proposal for the execution of a criminal, this controversy raises its head like in the recent hanging of Yakub Memon, accused of killing more than 250 people in Mumbai. Human rights activists become very active without appreciating the socio-legal framework of India.

The purpose of punishment as per jurisprudence is not to offend public conscience but to secure social justice. Reformative approach is the object of criminal law in India but not in cases of accused persons who can create terror in society and can disturb the social fabric of peace and tranquillity. Death penalty or capital punishment is provided for offences under Sections 120B, 121,132, 194, 302, 303, 305, 364A, 396 and 376A of the Indian Penal Code and Section 31A of the NDPS Act. However, the Supreme Court has liberalized the capital punishment in its so many judgments and has held that it can be given only in "rarest of the rare cases". Some such rarest of rare cases were exemplified as honour killing, police brutality in the form of encounter killing, killing by terrorists and rape with murder. *(Bachan Singh* Vs *State of Punjab (1980) (2 SCC 864).* The killing by terrorists and rape-cum-murder are punished with death penalty rightly so as society's conscience is threatened by such heinous crimes like in cases of the 26/11 attack on Mumbai and the subsequent hanging of terrorist Kasab and death penalty given to the accused in the famous Nirbhaya rape cum murder case.

The accused person condemned to death plays hide and seek game with law. After his death sentence is confirmed by the respective High Court, the condemned prisoner moves a mercy petition before the Governor. If that is cancelled, he moves the High Court and then the Supreme Court. If the Supreme Court rejects his appeal, he again goes in for mercy plea before the President of India. After his mercy petition is rejected by the President, he again goes to the Supreme Court because as per the observation of the Supreme Court, the President does not have any prerogative clemency power. Earlier it was considered final as the use of powers by the Governor and the President of India and the matter was beyond a review by the Courts.

As per figures by National Law University, Bangalore, only 71 executions have taken place after India's independence whereas a large number of condemned prisoners are languishing in jails after the award of death sentence on some ground or the other.

In India, the conviction rate was only about 16% in rape cases and about 27% in murder cases in the year 2012 as per the Crimes Records Bureau of the Ministry of Home Affairs. However, many crime cases even of heinous nature like murder and rape are not registered at police stations. Out of the registered cases, investigation is done only in 72.8 % of the IPC cases and the rate of case disposal by courts is as low as 13.2 per cent.

In such a scenario, India rightly opposed in 2012 a resolution of the United Nations General Assembly to abolish death penalty This is still the policy of the Government of India.

There are many instances wherein murder convicts jumped the parole and committed many other murders. In jail also, repentance or remorse is not observed by many rape-cum-murder convicts. In such a situation, it is also not prudent that the death penalty be abolished in India which is the law of the land.

1-15, September, 2015, Bureaucracy Today

♦♦♦

72

Status of Ken-Betwa Rivers Link

High profile project of linking of Ken-Betwa rivers concerning the Bundelkhand region, is being held up because of submergence of a national park in Panna district due to proposed Daudhan dam in Madhya Pardesh. An alternative free from such clearance could be pursued in consultation with the Secretary, Ministry of Environment & Forests so that delay at a later stage in securing requisite clearances may be avoided. A meeting is also scheduled to resolve the various issues raised by UP & MP on DPR of K-B link. Status note highlighting Ken-Betwa link proposal, Dam site selection, benefits to Bundelkhand region and Environmental issues and their mitigation measures are furnished below:

1. Ken-Betwa Link Project Proposal

The Ken-Betwa link envisages diversion of surplus water of Ken basin to water deficit Betwa basin. The link project will make feasible by way of substitution, the three projects in the Upper Betwa basin which were earlier not feasible hydrologically. These projects are Makodia dam, Barari, and Kesari barrages in the Upper reaches of the Betwa basin. Besides, the project is also to irrigate enroute areas and the command area envisaged under the proposed Ken Multipurpose-Project of Madhya Pradesh. A 77 m high dam, namely Daudhan is proposed across river Ken, about 2.5 Km upstream of existing Gangau Weir. The gross storage capacity of the dam is 2853 Mcum. Two power houses, one at the foot of the dam and other at the end of 1.1 Km long lower level tunnel are also proposed to generate power. The total installed capacity of both the power houses is 78 MW. The total length of the link canal will be 221 Km including 2 Km of tunnel.

As per the Detailed Project Report (DPR), surface water yield of Ken river at proposed Daudhan dam site at 75% dependability was assessed as 6590 Mcum. After accounting all kinds of upstream and downstream needs, surplus water available for diversion through the link is 1074 Mcum annually, out of which 591 Mcum is proposed for transfer to Betwa basin in the upstream of Parichha Weir and 366 Mcum will be utilised in the enroute command to irrigate 0.60 lakh ha area. The link will also provide 49 Mcum of water for drinking water supply to towns/villages lying enroute of link canal. It is estimated that 68 Mcum will be the transmission losses. Apart from enroute command, the command area of 2.41 lakh ha. is envisaged under the KMPP (Ken Multi Purpose Project) proposal of MP and intensification of existing ken command of 2.13 lakh ha in UP lying in Banda district and being irrigated through Bariarpur headworks. Out of 591 MCM (Million cubic meters) water proposed to be diverted in Betwa 273 MCM of water can be utilised by way of substitution through three proposed projects viz. Makodia dam, Kesari and Barari barrages for irrigating 0.62 lakh ha. in Upper Betwa sub-basin. In addition 13 Mcum of water will be provided for drinking water supply from Upper Betwa projects.

2. Benefits of Project to Bundelkhand Region

The Bundelkhand Region comprises 13 districts in total out of which 6 districts namely Datia, Tikamgarh, Chhatarpur, Panna, Sagar, and Damoh situated in Madhya Pradesh and Lalitpur, Jhansi, Jalaun, Hamirpur, Mahoba, Banda and Chitrakoot districts are in Uttar Pradesh. Four command area are being covered under Ken-Betwa link project, such as Enroute Command, Upper Betwa Command, Ken Command (MP) & Ken Command (UP). The link canal project will benefit total CCA

(Cultivable Command Area) of 557510 ha. with 697891 ha. annual irrigation under the four commands. Out of these four commands, three commands will benefit six districts of Bundelkhand region such as:

1. The enroute command of Ken-Betwa link lies in Chhatarpur and Tikamgarh districts of Madhya Pradesh and Mahoba and Jhansi districts of Uttar Pradesh. The cultural command area of 60294 ha. is covered through the enroute of the link canal.
2. The Ken command area (MP) lies in Chhatarpur and Panna districts of Madhya Pradesh. The CCA under this command is 241306 ha. and annual irrigation is 323350 ha.
3. The Ken command (UP) will stabilize the CCA of 213610 ha. area with the annual irrigation of 252017 ha. in Banda district.

Thus the total 515210 ha. CCA with 635661 ha. annual irrigation will be benefited to the Bundelkhand region through the Ken-Betwa link canal project. The project will also provide the drinking water facilities to the 13.5 lakh population in the Bundelkhand region. The Ken - Betwa link project has been included in the list of National Projects as approved by the Government of India.

To obtain above benefits, the construction of Daudhan dam is necessary. Though there are involvement of some environmental issues, such issues may be resolved in national interest by providing the suitable mitigational measures. It is to be stated here that environmental issues involved are not unusual in Ken-Betwa link but almost in each multipurpose projects. Suitable mitigation measures are necessary to be inbuilt in EIA and R&R Plan. This project, if successful, will pave way for implementation of other rivers linking project in India.

[Veerangana 2013, An annual publication of Bundelkhand Vikas Parishad, New Delhi]

♦♦♦

73

'I am a Businessman'

This statement by Prime Minister Narendra Modi is worth consideration. People in his home State, Gujarat, have a business mentality. Gujarat has established an example of unprecedented progress with this approach. Is the same approach relevant at our national level?

A businessman is one who keeps a proper account of profit and loss. In the present age of globalization, all multinational companies are surging ahead with this parameter. Where there is no profit or margin in a product or business, they either close that business or transfer their factories where raw material and labour are cheap and market is close by but one can neither change the geographical limit of a country nor can displace its people. Therefore, all parameters of the business cannot be applied to a nation.

As such, the business mentality is not bad. The *Bhagwad Gita* pronounces:

"vyavasayatmika buddhir ekeha kurunandana.." (Chapter II, *Shloka* 41).

"...vyavasayatmika buddhih samadhau na vidhiyate" (Chapter II, Shloka 44)

Hai Arjun! Those who are attached with pleasure and power or whose minds are drawn by that, have no business like intellect. It means that the people indulging in power and pleasure do not have resolute and one-point intellect. They act impulsively. They surrender the mind to a chosen goal and work coolly and speedily. They should identify their goal with the goal of the organization as per principles of management. This is called business intellect.

In the context of a nation, the main goal is "the welfare of the maximum people." The businessman has to associate himself with society.. He cannot do business in vacuum. If his neighbour is poor, he cannot remain rich for a long time. The economic mechanism should be so much legitimate that the common man feels that justice is being done to him. To guard against the increasing disparity, the Companies Act, 2013 has provided for a 2 per cent expenditure of the three-year average profit by ₹ 500 crore companies and the bigger ones towards their Corporate Social Responsibility (CSR):

The late Prime Minister, Mrs Indira Gandhi, was a symbol of expeditious decisions in spite of all hurdles but in the process she left a corrupt and inefficient government machinery. During the *Mahabharat,* Duryodhan and Shakuni used to make elaborate plans but Krishna and Arjun negatived their plans by constant actions. A businessman as Prime Minister can never allow his government funds to be released for his works in a new financial year after the lapse of six months when inadequate time will be left for the implementation of his schemes even at the cost of firing some of his officers or institutions.

In a country, one cannot tinker with the social, religious, literary and cultural fields with selfish motives because these fields are also engaged in nation building in their own way. One cannot neglect small things. Agricultural production cannot increase substantially unless a large number of landless farmers are also taken into the mainstream of development process by giving them land and security of tenure. In China and Japan, more than 90 per cent of the landless people have been given land by the Government. On this basic foundation, these countries have achieved unprecedented progress in the World today. In India, only about 28 percent' of the landless farmers have been provided land by the Government. If these people in rural India and the homeless in urban areas are not taken care of, they will run over the creations of globalization like Malls.

However, one cannot justify the constantly loss making industries or government undertakings to continue just to clear jobs for their employees because as a result the whole economy may collapse. But employment generating schemes with asset creations have to continue for the majority of the poor population in the rural areas because the business in India will be stabilized and strengthened only due to their purchasing power .

1-15, Nov. 2014, Bureaucracy Today

◆◆◆

Do not dwell in the past; do not dream of the future, concentrate the mind on the present moment.

– Buddha

74

Call for Performance of Duties

The Republic Day reminds citizens their duties under the Constitution of India.

Rights and duties are two sides of a coin. According to Gandhiji, "The source of right is duty. If we all discharge our duties, rights will not be far to seek. If leaving duties unperformed we run after rights, they will escape us."

The Constitution of India has provided fundamental rights to all citizens/persons in India *i.e.* right to equality, right to freedom including free speech and expression, rights against exploitation, right to freedom of Religion, cultural and educational rights, right to constitutional remedies. The Supreme Court has added few more rights through interpretation in various judgments like right to life, right to fair and speedy tried, right to health, right to livelihood to work and even right to development. Other rights can make the life more meaningful and worth living like prisoner's right to have necessities of life, right to women to be treated with decency and dignity, right to privacy, right to go abroad, right against custodial violence, right to health and medical aid of workers, right to reputation, right to freedom from noise pollution, right of hearing etc. However, there are corresponding eleven fundamental duties in the new Article 51 (A). The first and foremost duty assigned to every citizen of India is to abide by the Constitution and respect its ideals and institutions, the National flag and the National Anthem.

GOVERNED BY THE CONSTITUTION

We are all governed and guided by this Constitution irrespective of caste, religion, race, sex etc. Each citizen must therefore not only refrain from any such activity but also do his best to prevent any miscreant trying to show disrespect to our national symbols. Every nation is proud of its citizens because of their dedication, sincerity and patriotism. We, the citizens of India, have to be equally proud of our nation, our Constitution, our Flag and our Anthem.

We must put the nation above our narrow personal interests and then only we will be able to protect our hard-earned freedom and sovereignty. Secondly, the citizens of India must cherish and follow the noble ideals which inspired the national struggle for freedom. Thirdly, we should protect the sovereignty, unity and integrity of India, is a pre-eminent national obligation of all citizens of India. In a democratic system of governance, sovereignty lies with the people. To defend our sovereignty is our own responsibility.

Fourthly, citizens at large play a most vital role in a variety of ways, civilians may be required also to take up arms in defence of the country, if the situation warrants it. By fighting to defend the country, the citizens are fighting only to defend the own liberty and that their posterity. The citizens will have to come forward if required by the State. Fifthly the citizens should promote harmony and the spirit of common brotherhood amongst all the people of India transcending religious linguistic and regional or sectional diversities derogatory to dignity of women.

FUNDAMENTAL DUTIES

Spirit of brotherhood should come very normally among the citizens of a country like India where the norm has been to consider the entire world as one family. The Constitution also casts upon us the Fundamental Duty of ensuring that all practices derogatory to the dignity of women are renounced. Sixthly, we should preserve the rich heritage of our composite culture and preserve communal harmony is another Fundamental Duty of every citizen. It becomes the ardent duty of every citizen to ensure that these monuments and pieces of art are not in any way damaged, disfigured, scratched or subjected to vandalism or greed of unscrupulous traders and smugglers.

In the face of menace of the increasing pollution and environmental degradation, it is the duty of every citizen to protect and improve natural environment including forests, lakes, rivers and wild life and to have noise pollution and large-scale denudation of protests is causing immense harm to all human life on earth. The mindless and wanton deforestation in the names of the needs of development is causing havoc in the form of natural calamities and imbalances. By protecting our forest cover planting new trees, cleaning rivers, conserving water resources, reforesting wasteland, hills and mountains and controlling pollution in cities, villages and industrial units can help save the future of our fellow citizens and of planet earth itself. What is needed is a concerted effort forward through voluntary citizen initiatives. One of our great Founding Fathers, Jawaharlal Nehru always laid great emphasis on the need for Indian citizens developing a scientific temper and a spirit of inquiry - an inquisitiveness for learning from developments around the world.

It is the bounden duty of every citizens to preserve and promote a scientific temper and a spirit of inquiry to keep pace with the fast changing world. Also, they are tempered with a sense of humanism because ultimately the end of all progress is the human being and the quality of life and relationships that is developed. It is most unfortunate that in a country which preaches non-violence to the rest of the world, we see from time to time spectacles of senseless violence and destruction of public property indulged in by a few of its citizens. This is why it became necessary to prescribe the responsibility "to safeguard public property and abjure violence" as a fundamental citizenship duty.

The tenth duty is the drive for excellence in all spheres of individual and collective activity demand of times and a basic requirement in a highly competitive world. Nothing but the best would have survival potential in tomorrow's world.

In Keshavananda Bharat Case (1973), the Supreme Court held that each religion made its contribution to enrich the composite Indian culture as a happy blend or synthesis. Our religious tolerance (this) received reflection in our constitutional scheme in appropriate cases, if non-observance of duty by one citizens can be established as violation of the right of another, appropriate remedy may be provided by courts in spite the Fundamental Duties are not enforceable generally in courts.

This would include respect for professional obligations and excellence. Whatever work we take up either as individual citizens or as groups, our effort should be directed to achieving the goal of excellence. Also, special emphasis is called for in the area of collective activity. As right to education is declared as fundamental rights, the parents who do not send their wards to schools are not responsible citizens. Every parent or guardian is to provide opportunities for education to his child or ward between the age of 6 and 14 years;

The purpose of incorporating the Fundamental Duties in the Constitution is to make the citizens aware of their social and economic obligations and to warn them to do and not to do certain things in the interest of their country, their fellow citizens and themselves. Even duty to vote should be included as fundamental duty. This will make our government truly representative. A man who does not think it worthwhile to exercise this as obligation as a voter, is strangely ignorant of the real basis of all prosperity that he has or hopes for and the real duty which rests upon him as a man of elementary morals.

A man who will not take the trouble to vote is a poor spirited fellow willing to live on the labours of others and to shirk an honorable obligation, to do his share in return.

The 'Swachh Bharat' movement launched by our Prime Minister Narendra Modi is to remind their duty to preserve and keep the environment around them clean. However a country specially of size of India cannot progress by governmental efforts.

A country progresses by the due awareness and performance of duties by its citizens.

Rural Linking Hinterlands, January 2016

♦♦♦

75

Swachh Bharat Mission takes India to a New Identity

The Swachh Bharat Mission has the aim to end the open defecation habit fully in the country by October 2,2019 which will be Mahatma Gandhi's 150th birth anniversary. The total estimated outlay for this purpose is ₹ 62,009 crore of which the Central Government will contribute about ₹ 19,000 crore. The project is a part of the National Urban Sanitation Policy, 2008. It has City Level Sanitation Plans and State Sanitation Concepts. It has the National Advisory and Review Committee headed by the Secretary of the Central Ministry of Urban Development. Mission Directorates will monitor the mission projects in the States. There are NGOs, panchayat bodies and wards or *mohalla* committees as per Part IXA of the Constitution of India to monitor the progress of work under the campaign.

During the five-year period, the Government plans to construct 12 crore toilets across India. It built 31.83 lakh toilets from April 2014 to January 2015 which was 25. 4 per cent of the target for 2014-15. Thus, it is a gigantic task to construct a toilet in every household in India. Secondly, it is a difficult task to change the habit and attitude of elderly people to use toilets in place of open spaces for defecation.

However, some best practices have come up across the country. Maharashtra's Navlewadi village suffering from the chronic deficit of water has built a 35,000 litre water tank and installed several pipelines for the purpose. Even the UNICEF

Report has recognized that seven villages in Rajasthan have stopped the open defecation practice. Residents of Chauras village on the banks of the Narmada river in Madhya Pradesh have cleared the garbage. They have now clean drinking water and have stopped defecating in the open. The people of Puzhakhal in the Thrissur city of Kerala have installed waste bins and set up a biogas plant making it an ideal village for solid waste management. In one village in Kerala inhabited mostly by tribals, school students have brought bricks to construct the remaining toilets. In the most backward Koraput district of Odisha, 500 households in 11 villages of tribals have started using individually constructed toilets which was an alien practice to them. Darora village in UP got inspired by a children's song to make it free from open defecation and thereby free from disease. Gondwal's villagers in Ludhiana, Punjab, have collected garbage for decomposition and restored the greenery of the village. Similarly, in Haryana's Dontker village, women have demanded toilets from their husbands by singing: *"My dear beloved, please build a toilet in my house."*

COMPETITION

In the same vein, there is a re-emergence of competition to keep one's city clean. According to a survey, Mysuru has been named the cleanest city of the State after the launch of the Swachh Bharat Abhiyan. Damoh in M.P was called the dirtiest. In Delhi, one officer is tagged with each public toilet to monitor its cleanliness by the Municipal Corporations at least twice a day. Thus innovative solutions and initiatives are coming forth to make the clean India campaign a success.

However, more attention is required to be given to places of visit by foreign tourists who are a great source of foreign exchange to India. This will help to remove the tag of a dirty nation. The Railways are the forerunner of lifestyle practices in India. Therefore utmost care is to be taken by the Railways to keep their outfits clean beyond the cost-benefit analysis. Things do not seem much improved in the Railways as regards sanitation. However, far-off railway stations are better maintained now than the ones near Delhi which is the power centre of India.

In the case of urban areas, there are a large number of good schemes for local bodies to execute schemes for solid waste management with government subsidies. But the urban local bodies are not taking the due initiative forgetting the fact that in future they will not find places to collect garbage and have recycling schemes thereon.

16–30, November, 2016, Bureaucracy Today

◆◆◆

What you get by achieving your goals is not as important as what you become by achieving your goals.

— Goethe

76
On Karma

In the Bhagwad Gita, Lord Krishna has shown us a way to fight out in life without resources like Pandvas in Kurukshetra and in the situation of confusion and distress like of Arjun. We are more or less in the same situation everyday and we face the same predicament every moment.

The Gita asks us to carve out our way through the path of Karmayoga. This is the simplest and the fastest way. A man even with meagre or no resource can access success through Karmayoga.

The central theme of Karmayoga in the Gita is said to be contained in the following phrase;

कर्मण्येवाधिकारस्ते मा फलेषु कदाचन (Chapter II, verse 47)

It holds that if action or Karma or work is performed without the desire or hope of fruit, it will be the perfect action and will cause achieve success because then it will free the person from attachment or jealousy or hatred that is रागद्वेष :...

This action then, will be for good of all and purify him as karta or the doer as it will take, away his 'ego' 'अहम्' in the process. It will also make him above or relieve him from victory - defeat, distress - happiness, cold-hot, praise or criticism and will keep him in proper equilibrium of mind.

Even the Gyanis or persons involved in pursuit of knowledge or self-realisation, have to first start their process-meditation (sadhna) from Karma otherwise they will not be able to know what to get rid of. Even persons engaged or engrossed in worship or Bhakti (भक्ति/भक्ति) have to perform basic karma or action before getting fully absorbed in devotion to their ultimate (इष्ट) or lord.

But Karma or work is not something, which a person can avoid like his daily chores of activities on individual development.

The verse 5 in Chapter III read as :

न हि कश्चित्क्षणमणि जातु तिण्ठत्यकर्मकृत ।
कार्यते ह्वश : कर्म सर्व : प्रकृतिजैर्गुणै ।

How can a person do Karma when he finds obstacles around when he steps out of his home.? To this query the replies inherent in the Gita which talks thoroughly to have "समता" or equality or harmony in all walks of life. It says that one should perform his duty but he should not obstruct in performance of other's duty. It also exhorts everybody to fight against injustice even against own relatives, friends or even teachers. Arjuna fought for dharma as per his friend's advice. In fact, Krishna in his childhood organised milkmates without resources and overthrew the mighty unjust regime of Kansa.

All these paths lead towards "good for all" that is वसुधैव कुटम्बकम. Thus, there is no basic contradiction amongst the great men who have guided the people to make this world a better place to live in.

♦♦♦

77

The Bhagvad Gita: A Book of Battlefield

The Bhagvad Gita is a great book which takes one from sadness to happiness, from confusion to clarification and from worry to victory in war. None likes war but if one is placed in a battlefield, one has to fight the war.

Arjun, the warrior was placed in a situation of war. When he saw that there were his relatives, friends and teachers, he got disillusioned and went into depression as to for whom he will fight that war. Any result will be disastrous on both side. Hardly, any person will be left behind to enjoy the fruits or results of war. He even offered to quit the world and confine himself in solitude where he would be satisfied if someone provides him food to survive and water to drink. But his compatriot Krishna as driver of his chariot told him that there was no scope of fleeing from the battlefield or the world. The enemies would pursue him, trace him and will murder him in cold blood after taking him out of his place of hiding. There is no place in life to run away from one's dharma or duty. None would believe that he had left the battlefield on his own volition. Thus, he would also be defamed for that act even after his death as a cowardice.

Krishna says: "People will recount your perpetual dishonor/cowardice and to the honoured, dishonor is worse than death.[1]

---

1. Partha Sarathy, A: Bhagvad Gita, Chapter II: 34, Page 104 .

The great chariot-warriors will think that you have withdrawn from the battle out of fear and you that were highly esteemed by them will be lightly held.[2]

And your enemies will say many unbecoming words caviling your powers. What indeed could be more painful then that? Thus, if war that comes unsought should be fought as a righteous act which is an open door to heaven.

> According to the Bhagvad Gita, a person cannot avoid work like his daily chores of activities. The verse 5 in Chapter III holds that the possession of a body and limbs binds one with the compulsion of doing some work or the other all the time, voluntarily or involuntarily. If one doesn't do positive work, negative work will be done on him. The aim of action should be only to fulfil one's obligation and not satisfaction of one's desire. However, if one does work properly, both are automatically fulfilled.

The 'Bhagvad Gita' takes you from the situation of battlefield to the life situation. It enjoins that one not only should do one's duty without caring for its fruits, but he should do his duties expeditiously through quick decision making process and in a business like manner. Delay of split second in taking decision in responding to enemy's fire may cost life to the warrior.

Thus, there has to be single pointed determination. If this is not done, the intellect waives and seeks worldly diversion. It means that one should concentrate on his own duties and should not grab the duties of other persons. This is very dangerous and should be avoided.

The 'atman' or indweller is indestructible. Therefore one has not to bother about the death. 'Weapons do not cleave. This, nor fire burns. This, nor water wets. This, nor wind dries.[3]

"Just as a man casting off worn-out garments puts on new ones, so the embodied casting off worn-out bodies enters new ones."[4]

---

2. *Ibid,* Ch. II : 35.
3. *Ibid,* Ch. II : 23 P. 91.
4. *Ibid* : Ch.II: 22 P. 89 .

This is the sermon of the Bhagvad Gita which has enthralled soldiers to give away their lives which is otherwise not an easy thing. It is easier to say than it is done. But the Gita asks you to sacrifice for a righteous cause.

The Bhagvad Gita further says, "certain is death for the born and certain is birth for the dead, therefore, you should not grieve over the inevitable.[5]

Krishna further explains that it is not the relatives nor teachers nor other kinsmen for whom you should grieve. In fact those who have to die, are already dead. Krishna showed it in his universal form through his mouth that all those were already dead. "The wise grieve neither for the living nor for the dead" None of us will remain immortal. This Indweller in the bodies of all is ever indestructible. Therefore you should not grieve for any creature."[6]

"If you will not wage the righteous war, then having abandoned your duty and fame you will incur sin."[7] Dishonour is worse than death. For a publicly renowned person, loss of his honour and fame causes him more pain than death would. Therefore, they should prepare for the worst from the very beginning. In death except in suicide or cowardice death, one doesn't lose his name and fame whereas he loses them by abandoning his obligatory duty. Therefore, death is welcome in the Indian Culture as one of the religious rites or Samskara.

Similarly, heat and cold, pleasures and pains come and go. They are impermanent. The only permanent thing is the righteousness or truth reflected through one's duty or *Dharma*.

The duty (ordained spiritually or by custom) of one, even though devoid, of any appealing quality, is much better than that of another's duty no matter howsoever well performed. It is better even to die doing one's own duty; for taking on the duty assigned to another is full of grave danger.

5. *Ibid* : Ch.II: 27 P. 96.
6. *Ibid* : Ch.II: 30 P. 100.
7. *Ibid* :a Ch.II: 33 P. 03.

Even the inconvenient duties of one, which are devoid of merit, are preferable to more convenient ones of another, for the actions enjoined by natural aptitude never involve one in evil consequences.

To perform one's duty properly, one should have steady wisdom like a successful wrestler who is very quick in action but is very cool in his mind to know the next step of his opponent to give him a befitting reply.

A steady wisdom person is one whose mind is not agitated by sorrow nor is excited by joy and is free from desire, fear and anger.[8]

If one is agitated during war, the delusion will arise, from delusion confusion of memory will result and from confusion of memory, loss of intellect and from loss of intellect, he perishes[9]

The steady wisdom it is more relevant in modern warfare where the wars are fought more by intellectual gadgets and armaments rather than traditional weapons of swords, guns etc. This is the time to aim at the enemy with a mathematical accuracy to know his strengths and weaknesses and to target him rightly.

To achieve this level of peace and steadfastness of intellect, one has to be a self controlled person away from desires and he should be awake when others are sleeping.

One who does not discipline the mind nor has the senses under control, cannot have a steady fast and single-pointed intellect. With a diffused intellect clear perception is impossible. Without clear perception, diverse thoughts keep buffetting the mind. Peace eludes a buffeting mind. When there is no peace of mind how can one hope for any happiness? This is the picture of all people in the world who spend their lives controlling and disciplining others but have no time to control or discipline their own minds.[10]

---

8. *Ibid* : Ch. 11:56 P. 132
9. *Ibid* : Ch. 11:63 P. 141
10. *Ibid* Ch. II: 66 Page 65.

It is also important to know one's enemy outside after winning the enemy inside. Excess of eating, of fasting, of sleeping and of keeping awake are hindrances in performance of the job with the yogic concentration and efficiency. Similarly, the Sattwic likes following food.

Easily digestible foods generally promote longevity, pure foods like fruits, dry fruits, milk and milk products fall in this category, foods such as wheat, butter, barley and grapes, promote physical and mental vigour, vegetables and fruit juices promote health and prevent diseases, foods like sweets in moderate quantities, dry fruits and fruits promote happiness and cheerfulness, milk, fruit juices and the like are generally appetising and are easily digestible, oily substances like butter, ghee and vegetable oils keep the body system cool, these are substances which, being easily assimilable, give nourishment to the body and help it fight diseases and keep mind and senses in control and in unison with the intellect. Moderate quantities of sweets and snacks promote the flow of digestive juices and are considered to be agreeable. Bitter, sour, salty, excessively hot, pungent, dry and burning foods are to the natural liking of a Rajasic person; such foods produce pain, grief and disease. Stale, tasteless, putrid and rotten foods and those which are left over and are impure are liked by Tamasic person.

Thus, one can know his enemy from his food habits if he can gather such information.

The basic purpose of life is happiness. People fight the battle to make this world a better place for living by eliminating the wicked or the Trouble Creators. In Chapter 18, Krishna tells Arjuna, "True happiness is like poison in the beginning but is nectarine in the end. That which is like nectar in the beginning and poisonous in the end is false happiness[11]". Thus fighting, battle or the battle of life may seem to be difficult in the beginning but after winning it, it gives the profound satisfaction for having performed one's duty and consequential happiness.

11. ROW, JAYA : Profile of the Perfect Person, 'Page 48.

But one has to prepare himself first physically as well mentally to fight the battle. For that, one has to have disciplined mind.

"Sense enjoyment is not forbidden. It is an inherent aspect of human life. But if you allow it to carry on unsupervised, you will get destroyed. The famous picture of the horse chariot from the Kathopanisad conveys this idea. The five horses represent the senses. The reins are the mind. The charioteer is the intellect. When the charioteer is alert and skilful, the reins guide the horses in the direction determined by the charioteer. Then he reaches his destination. If the charioteer lacks the requisite skills and is not on guard, the reins are loose, the horses go whichever way they please and the chariot crashes. If one doesn't tread on this path step by step one will meet the result of self annihilation.

Thus, one should avoid those 'gunas' or qualities which may result into his destruction. When one is full of Sattawaguna, there is a feeling of perfect contentment, peace and enlightenment in mind. The tendency to acquire objects of worldly and sensor enjoyment, or to increase those already acquired, is called Rajguna. Tamoguna is the quality of inertia which is manifested on the form of delusion, aversion to duties and indulgence in meaningless activities.

One should not be over ambitions to rule the world or desire to be the ruler or the policeman of the world and enforce his way of thinking or discipline others. One should rather show his self example to guide others to follow him. But if one is placed in a battlefield by dint of misdeeds or accidents or circumstances created by the enemy, one should face with all his might. Mahatma Gandhi, being the apostle of non-violence, never hesitated to support the Indian Army to fight the invasion by the Pakistan Army in Kashmir just after the independence. Acquiescence or inaction in the enemy's egoistic or violent action is no 'dharma' or 'duty' or spirituality. It is a straightforward cowardice.

Lord Krishna exhorts Arjuna to rise up, win glory, conquer the enemies and enjoy royal affluence. They have already been slain by Me, be you merely an instrument.

In this well-known shloka, the Lord explains how the duties in the world are to be performed. For this, He gives three directions.

(*i*) By this the Lord does not instruct Arjuna to perform his actions with a view to gaining fame; He points out to Arjuna how to avail of the glory which would naturally be his by performance of his duties as an instrument of the Lord.

(*ii*) In shloka 37 of chapter III, the Lord has pointed out that desires and anger caused by the thwarting of desires are the real enemies of a person in this world. Besides anger, avarice is also a modification of desires which is caused by their unfulfillment. The trio of desires, anger, and avarice causes delusion. These are, in fact, the real enemies of a human being and in this shloka the Lord exhorts Arjuna to conquer them.

(*iii*) Territory, Wealth, Properties and the like are generally regarded as constituting the affluence of a kingdom. Here this word has been used in a symbolic manner. To pursue desires arising in the mind leads to bondage and slavery. To conquer and master them enables one to rule over the kingdom of Selfhood and one enjoys its affluence.

This book of battlefield is much more relevant today because now-a-days wars are fought on all fronts from the farmer's field, factories to the battlefield. And it is fought by the diplomats and the soldiers equally. Even soldiers or warriors have to be of scientific temper as targets are very sophisticated and are aimed with sophistication and buttons involving lot of mathematical, scientific and intellectual calculations. A single point mistake may cause havoc. A mistake of one degree in targeting the enemy may cause loss of thousands or lacs of innocent lives by dropping a powerful bomb, chemical releases or a nucleus device. Every instrument is a sophisticated one and is more based on soldier's or warrior's intellectual calculation rather than his physical strength or valour. Similarly, a man has to fight number of multifarious enemies within who were not there in earlier times.

The Bhagvad Gita ordains the ways and means one should fight in the battlefield of life as well as in the actual battlefield. Let us all emulate this great book which will make our World a better place to live.

REFERENCES

Agrawal, Dr. Pramod Kumar - Bhgvad Gita : Natya Roop, Published by Pitambra Books Pvt. Ltd. B - 95, Industrial Area, Bijaui, Jhansi (U.P.) Year 2007 (2nd Edition, Total page, 345)

Partha Sarathi - Bhagvad Gita, Published by A Partha Sarathy, 1A Land Sand, Mumbai- 400006. Year 2008, Total Page, 868

Row, Jaya - Profile of the Perfect Person, Published by Jaico Publishing House, A-2, Jash Chambers, 7-A Sir Phirozshah Mehta Road, Fort, Mumbai-400001, year 2011, Total Pages 139

16-31, March , 2013, Business Economics

♦♦♦

78

Strategy to Tackle Naxalism

Naxalism is the biggest challenge to the internal security of India. A day doesn't pass when an incident of violence by Naxalites is not reported. Naxalism is causing more casualties yearly than the terrorist violence in Jammu & Kashmir and militancy in the North Eastern States.

The Government had been fighting a pitched battle with various groups of Naxalites for five decades but the problem has persisted. In fact, the total number of incidents and number of casualties has been continuously increasing. Very recently the number of causalities has reduced despite increasing of Naxal attacks. Therefore, people in general have a genuine cause for concern about how the Naxalite violence can be reduced if not eliminated permanently.

Due to the widening net of Naxalite violence, the common man in India feels threatened. Where there is injustice, violence will be its natural fallout, sooner or later. If an equitable or egalitarian society is established in the true sense, there will be peace. The equity can be achieved either by liberal releases of funds, goods and services by the State or by equitable redistribution of properties in society. In rural India, most of the properties are locked in landed properties. Therefore, land reform for equitable re-distribution of land is required. No government can afford to make state largess available to about 40 crore i.e. 400 million rural poor.

Land reform is the plank that can take the country into the group of developed countries. China has distributed its 90% arable land among about 90% landless families or households. In Japan 41% of available,. arable land has been distributed among the 81% landless families. India as per an estimate by Roy Prosterman of Rural Development Institute and University of Washington. USA, has distributed only about 5% land among less than 28% of the landless population. Thus, there is a wide gap of inequality existing in India.

When the need for land reform is projected before the bureaucrats or politicians concerned, there is lukewarm response. Bureaucrats in charge of implementation of land reforms either don't understand land reforms or they don't have any willingness to understand. Over and above, the police personnel as usual, assure to the bureaucrats and political bosses that they will soon overpower Naxalites and restore peace in society, which never happens. The political executives don't want to venture into implementing land reforms, because first, their field level cadres or supporters either don't appreciate the benefits of land reforms in the long run or they don't want to disturb the status quo in rural India though rural society is perched on a volcano of unrest. The Naxalites, while spreading their cult of violence, project such cases of palpable injustice and discrimination before the downtrodden people and assure them to undo long injustice caused to them with their armed might. The simple and innocent poor villagers are easily carried away by their propaganda. A section of villagers who do not toe their line, are either threatened or victimized and do not find any protection from the local police in the face of threat of Naxalites in villages. Accordingly, they also succumb to their influence.

The rural poor only know cultivation. If they are put back into cultivation, they will not starve. If they are evicted from cultivation due to land acquisition, they will be jobless and will swell the ranks of the poor after the hefty compensation received by them for their dear land is exhausted. Therefore, there is so much agitation by the land evictees against tinkering with the new favourable Land Acquisition Act.

It is a fact that the police in various states are trying their best to tackle Naxalite violence. Para-military forces have been deputed in large numbers by the Central Government in the affected states to prevent violence by the Naxalites. There is some success here and there. At present, Naxal violence has come down. Many Naxalites have surrendered yet the problem re-appears in some other states in aggravated form. Andhra Pradesh has controlled the Naxal violence by creating new specialized command forces specialized in jungle warfare named Grey Hounds. However the problem has not been completely eliminated. But in Andhra Pradesh also, the counter-violence by police and Grey Hounds was accompanied with extensive land reform measures undertaken during the popular late Chief Minister R.S. Reddy. In West Bengal, there was no Naxal violence during 34 years of the Left Front government from 1977 to 2007 because the main agenda of the Left Front government was implementation of land reforms. It was noticed only from year 2008, when the Left Front Government gave priority to land acquisition for industrialization over land reforms. The flare-up thereby caused could not be controlled by the powerful Left Front government in West Bengal and it was ousted from power in the year 2011. Various state governments are trying to wean away the rural poor from the Naxal fold like the Chhattisgarh Government which has been providing rice in tribal areas at concessional rates and has a continuing deep rooted and sustained anti-Naxal campaign.

Similarly, implementation of STORFA, 2006 is a good step to ensure the right to land in the vicinity of forests under occupation by tribals and to ensure the right to collect minor forest produce like woodlots, fallen leaves and dry jungle seeds and flowers. However, concerted efforts have yet to be made so that there may be direct impact on the campaign against Naxalites who have also derailed from their main track of land reform. Naxalites nowadays are only engaged in countering the powerful state police force and they have been virtually left with no time or opportunity to follow to their main agenda to ensure land to the landless, the tiller, delivery of justice to the poor, etc.

If government surplus land is not available for distribution, the government should purchase land in the same village or neighbouring village where the landless poorest of the poor will go and cultivate the land and will save. himself and his family from starvation. The government .should distribute minimum 16 decimals per family for three tier cultivation starting from coarse grain cultivation and vegetable cash crops to fast growing trees as in Bangladesh.

In Jharkhand, government surplus ceiling land should be distributed among the landless persons, specially the tribals on priority. In Chhattisgarh, all lands including unsurveyed land of Abujmarh area in erstwhile Bastar district covering more than 5000 hectares should be surveyed and updated. Computerized land records should be made and distributed to all landowners and pattadars. In the State of Odisha, bataidars (share croppers) should be recorded on lands which have been cultivated by them on the promise or by convention to share produce. In Madhya Pradesh, the tribals living on the fringe of forests should be recorded and given the right to collect minor forest produce or dry leaves under the STORFA, 2006. Karnataka presents a scenario, where contract farming can be utilized for the advantage of the farmers whose lands have been given for contract farming. UP highlights a scene where land acquired for large public sector enterprises is still lying vacant inside the factory and is a source of problem for the units as well as for local people.

In Andhra Pradesh, land is required to be restored to the tribals which were illegally transferred to non-tribals. In Andhra Pradesh, Nyaya Panchayats at the block level or at the level of Panchayat Samities is an innovation worth emulation by other states. In Bihar, land records are almost non-existent, in spite of availability of requisite funds by the Central Government for the purpose. There is an urgent need for updating of land records and vesting of surplus lands in government belonging to erstwhile zamindars or jotedars. In West Bengal, a large quantum of land is locked in court cases especially at the High Court and the Supreme Court which can be distributed, if released from Courts, among the landless poor. In Maharashtra, lack of bank finance for the crops is the main cause of suicides by the farmers especially in the Vidarbha region of Maharashtra.

The police solution is underway in all affected States of India. There are some stories of success of the police operation like Grey Hounds in Andhra Pradesh, Auxiliary Armed Police Force in Chhattisgarh, killing of top Naxalite leader in a genuine police encounter in West Bengal, 40% recruitment in Central Paramilitary forces from border areas and areas affected by militancy or Naxalism. However, due 'political will' to solve the Naxalism problem by the State Governments has not yet been demonstrated.

Due to traditional anti-people working of police, the police action could not make perceptible change in the situation. There is more of blame game between the local police and deployed para-military forces, posting of unwilling officers in those areas rather than the cream of officers from the state police force, incidents of connivance of local police with Naxalites and lack of actionable intelligence information by local police set-ups and inadequate bank of knowledge about local inhospitable terrain with the local police. Even if all deficiencies are removed in the police set-up, it will not be able to solve the problem unless concerted efforts are made through implementation of land reform measures and development schemes in an impartial manner. Developmental schemes afflicted with corruption fuel the Naxalite agitation more than they solve. But development schemes cannot be stopped for that reason. There should be many times more vigilance on execution of developmental schemes in Naxal affected areas than elsewhere in the country. I am sure that the Indian administration led by political executives will awake and undertake implementation of land reform measures in the Naxal affected states on top priority basis.

16–30, November 2015, Business Economics

♦♦♦

79

Non-Government Sector is More Important

If we analyse the Union Budget for 2014-15, its total size comes to about ₹ 18 lakh crore, including the budget for India's defence and other paramilitary forces. And if we add the about ₹ 6,300-crore budget of the Railways and about ₹ 1.47 lakh crore budgets of all the State Governments, the total size of the government cake will be around ₹ 20 lakh crore. The size of India's GDP is about ₹ 100 lakh crore. Thus the Government impacts only on 20% of the Indian economy. This means that if India has to advance in the 21st century, it has to take care of its non-government sector more than the government one.

Like the government sector, the private sector is also afflicted with indecision, corruption and feudalism. Unless collective growth is allowed to flourish and merit is given its due place, the Indian private sector cannot compete with world class organizations or multinationals which exploit merit to accumulate profit. There is a need for professionalism at all levels in the private sector too. Familial organizations have, to show their relevance if they want to survive and flourish. At least, the private sector should not always blame the Government for not being able to give due output because of government policies or lack of proactive actions on the part of government machinery. It should first try to organize itself properly. The IT sector in India never blamed the Government after the economy was liberalized in the nineties and it has proved that it is not only the best in the World but the Indian youth is also the best in the world IT sector.

There is no denying that the Government should now be prepared to play the role of a facilitator in the economy rather than the main mover. The majority of India's population constituting farmers and small retail businessmen has nothing to do with the Government. The Government should ensure that those officials and political persons who adopt obstructive methods are properly dealt with. Police should give the private sector due protection for production and the Government should facilitate its regulatory requirements. If corruption comes in the way of national growth, it should be rooted out and should be eliminated under various anti-graft laws. Manufacturers or industrialists should not be viewed as tax evaders and black marketeers only.

Politicians should see to it that they do not occupy the space meant for NGOs/civil societies or men of arts, literature, culture, etc. Earlier in the Rajya Sabha 12 seats used to go to eminent persons in the fields of literature, science, art and social service. Now even 12 seats out of a total 780 Parliamentary seats are filled on political considerations. Padma and literary awards are arbitrarily decided. Even order for the purchase of books is approved by a political executive. However, the hon'ble President of India keeps patronizing efforts of civil societies and general citizens in nation-building.

CORRUPTION IN NGO

Efforts are on by the bureaucracy and the police to throttle the work done by NGOs. There is no denial that there is corruption in NGOs but that does not mean that the system of NGOs should be disbanded. It is observed that when a person acquires a ministerial berth, he starts nominating men from his household, constituency or party on all bodies wherever there is no defined qualification. Even semiliterate persons are nominated to literary or language bodies. As a result, the meritorious or specialized persons in that field get overlooked and mediocrity takes precedence over meritocracy. This unending chain will go on until the system breaks down. It is an accepted fact that the American "spoils system" is applicable in all democracies over the world, though to a limited extent. One of the reasons for such arbitrary or partial appointments to various government bodies is due to an unprofessional approach to the issue in the bureaucracy. The bureaucracy hardly maintains a data bank for each and every post or membership of government bodies, firstly because of its laxity and secondly, because its recommendations are not paid proper heed.

In spite of this, it is the prerogative of the political executive' to accept the recommendation or not. It is the solemn duty of the political executive to disagree with a file noting stating his cogent reasons. If entire responsibility is taken by the political elite with the help of the bureaucracy and the police; there will be an explosive situation. None can feed 125 crore people of India only on doles and subsidies. The need of the hour is that all Indians should contribute their best in nation-building. All sections of society should be given due space and opportunity to develop themselves. It will be an ideal day in Indian democracy if the Pradhan of a Gram Panchayat comes out of the furnace of the Indian system successfully and becomes the Prime Minister of the country.

1-15, August, 2014, Bureaucracy Today

♦♦♦

80

Currency Reflects Work Rendered by a Country's Citizens

Currency is a representation of a country's capital. Capital is the axis on which the world revolves, says Karl Marx. Generally a currency reflects the economic health of a country. Currency is legal tender money. It is also known as common money or ordinary money. It has national acceptability because it has a guarantee of the sovereign government through its central bank. It has also international acceptability because it is subject to interchangeability in other currencies of the world.

Five sources or factors affecting the money stock in India are more or less the same.

CREDIT TO GOVERNMENT

The net bank credit to the Indian Government is huge because there is no control on the sovereign government. Most of the governments, including that of India, issue currency notes recklessly to repay loans to their central banks. The only safety valves are that the Government should not use public funds for non-productive purposes. Secondly, the Government should avoid non- Plan expenditure.

CREDIT TO COMMERCIAL SECTOR

In India, the major chunk of bank credit is given to the commercial sector *i.e.* the non-governmental sector. Governments, including those of States and the Centre, are operating to effect only 17% of the GDP. Therefore, the commercial sector is the most important covering industries and the service sector. The private sector is to be blamed if the currency plunges internationally because the prices of raw material and machines are now uniform the world over. The exploitation of labour or extra work by labourers is the only panacea which can push an economy in this globalization era. Germany, Japan and China have come to the forefront of development. Germany was rebuilt after the devastation in the Second World War because its citizens worked for 18 hours by taking their salary for eight hours.

FOREIGN EXCHANGE ASSETS

The foreign exchange assets in India have been doing fine for a few years because the country's reserves are more than the liability of its foreign debt. Therefore, the problem of foreign debt is not haunting India which was the phenomenon in the first three decades after Independence in 1947. The falling rupee is increasing the cost of Indian imports like fuel and is decreasing the value of total exports.

GOVERNMENT'S LIABILITY TO THE PUBLIC

The Government's liability to the public is quite huge. This is a general phenomenon in the US and in all other developed countries though it should not go beyond a permissible limit of 22% of the GDP which is now more than double. As a result, when the public demand increases, every Government has to print notes or to crave for foreign currency through foreign direct investment (FDI) or else a price spiral takes place in the country. Another relief can be by way of receiving heavy remittances from NRIs.

It seems that due to cheap populist schemes and their inadequate implementation by panchayat bodies new assets are not being created in India. Secondly, the manufacturing and service sectors are not performing well. More positive work culture should be created and a more responsive conduct from citizens of the country is required so that they may stand on their own.

It is, therefore, essential that the Prevention of Money Laundering Act, 2002 and the FEMA, 1998 should be properly implemented so that politicians and black marketers are made liable for all their ills. The countrymen should also realize that the rupee can be strong if they work hard at their respective job places. The only solution is stable and continuous hard work by citizens of the country.

It is very awkward to see that the currencies of most of the countries cannot be exchanged worldwide. I am sure that by hard labour across the globe, all currencies will be equally exchangeable and respectable.

♦♦♦

81

Why Do Farmers Commit Suicide?

India's sixty percent population of farmers directly or indirectly depend upon agriculture. India's small farmers, once the country's economic backbone are increasingly suffering in the melee of globalization.

In normal times, one Indian farmer commits suicide every half an hour. Even suicide is rampant among the international community of farmers. The frequency of suicide increases when there is drought, flood or other unforeseen adversities like untimely rains or unfavorable change in seasons. As a result, there is drop in their farm income, *i.e.* they owe more than they earn. With limited resources, farmers depend on borrowed money to purchase seeds and other inputs like fertilizers and pesticides. The foodgrains, vegetables or cash crops prices do not increase in proportion to the price rise of the farm inputs. As a result, in spite of support prices by the government, the cost of production is more than the prices of inputs. A farmer first takes bank loan. When, he is unable to pay off these loans, he borrows from the money lenders at exorbitant rates of interest upto 36% to save his farm land which is dearest to him. Thus, he is in constant cycle of debt.

On the other hand, he has pressing health expenses, marriage of daughter and other family and social commitments. He has hardly any saving habit. As a result he has hardly any money for bad days. Opening of bank account has helped him to inculcate saving habit among farmers. As per a survey 86.5 percent of farmers, who took their own lives were financially indebted. The average debt of farmer was about ₹ 50,000/-. However, 60 percent had debt between ₹ 6600 to ₹ 33,000/- The government can save sixty percent farmers in the wake of crisis situation by waiving off land loans and by supporting them to pay off loans to the money lenders. The money lenders and sometimes banks exert lot of physical and mental torture on farmers. They are emotional people with simplicity and integrity as way of life. Therefore, they are driven to take extreme steps whereas the big industrialists travel in jets to head of government to request him to waive off their loans or give them government support which are many more times than the total loans of farmers.

In cotton belt of Vidarbha (Maharashtra), there are two suicides in a day whereas in the arid region of Bundelkhand in UP and M.P., the rate of suicide is even higher because this region is often affected by drought or low rains. As a result, continuous migration of farmers is observed from the region of Bundelkhand to metropolitan city of Delhi or agriculturally rich Punjab and Haryana for seasonal job. Even MNREGA scheme has not impacted perceptibly to reduce the migration of farmers from these areas facing recurring wrath of nature.

In India, more than one lakh farmers have taken their lives since 1997. After untimely rains and hailstone unleased in parts of Uttar Pradesh from March to April, 2015, about fifty farmers took their lives every day. This is a very sorry state of affairs and pose a great challenge before so called welfare governments at the Centre and in the State.

Long term solutions are to ensure irrigation facilities, quality seeds, fertilizers and pesticides and to link farmers with bank loans for each crop with subsidy at least in rate of interest. The overdose of chemical fertilizers and pesticides is to be stopped which render the soil infertile in long run which drive even rich farmers to suicide and cancer. There should be stringent penal measures against money lenders aided and abetted by the local musclemen who charge high rates of interest from the farmers. No perceptible action has been taken under the Money Lenders Act in any state. Therefore, the exploitation of farmers by them goes unabated. The norms to give government relief in cases of calamities, should be revised and the procedure should be made simpler and quicker. Officials indulging in corruption and inaction should be brought to book. The declaration by government should be prompt because declaration takes lot of time to get implemented and to reach to the farmers in the field. The crops of the farmers should be insured and payment of interim compensation should be within fifteen days of the loss of crop. The insurance premium of Crop Insurance Scheme should to a large extent be paid by government. There should be transparent system of purchase of output of farmers at madis, hats or foodgrains' purchase or procurement centres with minimum deductions towards unexplained charges etc. procurement. The panchayats should also mediate payment of loans between the money lenders and farmers sincerely. The farmers also need to adopt proper crop mix to avoid vagaries of nature.

◆◆◆

82

Problem of Intolerance: Causes and Cure

Intolerance is a world wide phenomenon in all continents and sub-continents. At some places, it is based on religion, race, caste, sex, descent, place of birth, residence or based on social or economic inequality. Indian culture and the Constitution have been advocating for tolerance but unfortunately India has also joined the wandwagon of those countries, societies or races which are affiliated with intolerance based on religious fundamentalism or fanaticism.

The incidents of intolerance are causing conflicts and bloodshed and is making society unstable and unpeaceful. This is suicidal for India.

The main causes are ideological differences which turn into real and serious conflicts. Second reason is glaring disparities in society which create latent ill will and hatred among different sections of the society. This is more accentuated when people find that state machinery instead of being impartial and objective, indulges into discrimination, corruption, favoritism and nepotism.

Similarly, demonstration of superior culture, development or military strength by nations generate hatred among not so developed societies. Crisis of high expectations in life and non-fulfilment of promises by the politicians create unrest.

Display of ill earned wealth causes disapproval. This simmering discontent suddenly explodes on any issue which makes public consensus though it may rationally be a non- issue.

They are guided by information which now reaches them unfiltered through social media or Internet. By the time facts come to light, damage has already done. Through these clashes of intolerances, people will like to assert their identities through religion, caste or community. The government rather than bringing truth in focus and starting the dialogue tries to suppress root causes specially under intoxication of the state police power and majority gained in election. This is more manifested in developing and undeveloped countries where rulers behave like dictators or martial law administrators.

As a result, simple causes of discrimination, exploitation or injustice result into huge violence and bloodshed taking thousands of innocent lives. In India there is a grand tradition of rulers like Ram, Ashok, Shivaji, Akbar, Maharani Laxmibai etc. who treated every citizen equally.

The solution is a long term one. People should follow the basic tenets of their religion which are based on love, compassion, harmony, co-operation, and assimilation. People should follow their culture and not civilization. Civilization creates sense of disparity and deprivation which is the order of the day so far it relates to lifestyle.

The cure lies in tolerance. While tolerance means not to interfere with other's ways of living or thinking. It is to bend before others and allow others to bend before you. It suggests responsiveness to the 'otherness' of the other. Thirdly, there is level jumping in the society. The highest class patronizes the lowest class of people to serve their vested interest of money and power. As a result, middle class is clueless which used to convince and keep disgruntled people in check. This middle class in society and middle level management in organizations is to be given their due role and responsibility. Dialogue instead of clash should be way of life. Fourthly, the State should ensure good governance and equal treatment. However, classification can be reasonable. Government instrumentality should not only be honest, impartial and just, it should also appear honest and impartial. As the faith of people will increase in government or state, the flare-ups due to religious discords or differences will be tackled without use of force. Government however, should penalize masses and should punish their officers and staff holding them responsible. Lastly, non-violence should be taught in schools and be made a part of life.

It is surprising how Islam intrinsically religion of brotherhood can be responsible for all the violence which is being done today in its name. There are four factors, the geopolitical and geo-strategic factors, the economic factors of poverty and under development, the ideologization of the religion, search of identity by Muslims in non- Islamic countries and last but not least the oblivion of the civilization factors in Islam. The Muslim community must take the extremists acts more seriously because of the negative consequences of terrorism on the future of Islam. The thinking Muslims without fear from radicalists will have to go out of the comforts of homes and offices and work in seminaries, mosques and other public places to acquaint common Muslims of the consequences of terrorist acts for the community.

The Hindus, following the advice of late Sarvapalli Radhakrishnan should abandon thinking that they are only possessors of light and others are groveling in darkness. Dalai Lama says that in human societies, there will always be differences of views and interests. The only way out is the promotion of a culture of dialogue and non-violence for the future of mankind. The Indian culture promotes "World is a Family". If religion creates conflicts, people will abhor religion in line with Karl Marx that religion is opium for masses.

According to Gandhiji, the indispensable condition of the social freedom and social welfare is the "tolerance of the diversities". It the "unity in diversity." What the Hindu philosophy and Vivekanand call "Advaita" meaning the essential unity of man. It implies co-operative relationship with all life rather then competitiveness. Indian culture offers its real solution. Constitution of India under Article 51A (e) asks every citizen to promote harmony and the spirit of common brotherhood amongst all the people of India transcending religious, linguistic and regional or sectional diversities. This is the only panacea for development of individual, community, the nation and the world.

Uday India, September 26, 2015

♦♦♦

> *Life's most persistent and urgent question is, 'What are you doing for others'.*
>
> **— Martin Luther King, Jr.**

83

Ambulance is the VIP

Respecting the common man's sentiments, the Government of India prohibited the use of the red light by all dignitaries from May 1, 2017. According to PM Modi, every Indian is a VIP. The Prime Minister, himself has discontinued using the red beacon. Thus, the Government has gone ahead with the Supreme Court's verdict in December 2013 in the *Abhay Singh vs Union of India* case where the apex court directed the Union and State Governments to amend their Motor Vehicle Rules so as to drastically curtail or restrict the use of the red light on the top of vehicles.

However, many VIPs with feudal mentality are still trying to bypass the spirit of the latest amendments in the Central Motor Vehicles Rules by using different types of horns which are similarly illegal under Rule 119 of the Rules and the Noise Pollution (Regulation and Control) Rules, 2000 and under the Environment Protection Act, 1986.

As per a notification of the Ministry of Home Affairs, traffic can be stopped only for the President, the Vice President and foreign dignitaries of the Prime Minister's status. In the US, traffic is halted for about 10 minutes for the powerful President. If 100 people have to wait for 10 minutes, it amounts to a wastage of the nation's 16 hours and 40 minutes. Mechanism is being devised so that traffic may be allowed for the common man with the least obstruction or problem. Under Article 19(l)(d) of the Constitution, every citizen has a right to move freely throughout the territory of India subject to reasonable restrictions in the public interest. Therefore, the use of an ambulance has been made an exception because life and death are more important than anything else. Thus, in the present scenario an ambulance is the real VIP and every citizen of India should make way for it in spite of little inconvenience to him as his constitutional and legal obligation.

It is observed that in spite of the well-laid-down provisions, police constables allow so called or self-imposed VIPs to pass through on roads violating traffic rules. This should be stopped in new India. Many a time, the poor constables allow VIPs even overlooking the ambulance fearing reprised by the VIP or by a officer who wants to please the VIP for his self-interest. However, this wrong practice can be stopped if a few police officials or constables are made accountable for the violation of traffic rules by VIPs either with or without the red beacon or horn and VIPs are made to pay fine for the violation of rules as the ambulance is the only VIP in the present set-up along with the President, the Vice President and the Prime Minister of India.

1–31, October, 2017, Bureaucracy Today

♦♦♦

84
Freedom of Press in India

Freedom of speech and expression is the bulwark of a democratic form of government. It includes the 'freedom of press' as contained in the American Constitution. Press in India includes print media, electronic media and even social media. In India freedom of press is not absolute. The various restrictions within which the press has to function can be categorised under two distinct heads.

First, there are legal limitations which include constitutional law, that is, Article 19(2), Municipal Acts and judicial pronouncements. Secondly, there are practical restrictions such as monopoly with regard to management and ownership, public opinion, communication facility and journalistic acumen etc.

The constitutional restrictions have been imposed in the interest of 'sovereignty and integrity' of India, security of the state, friendly relations with foreign states, public order, decency and morality, contempt of court, defamation, incitement to an offense or violence. Within these limitations, the Indian Press can criticise and condemn the government and its policies as much as it desires.

After the Constitution came into force, so many public Acts have been made so as to restrict the publications and circulations of newspapers. Out of those, certain provisions of Newspaper (Price & Page) Act, 1956 were challenged in the Supreme Court in 1962.

Examining the ambit of these provisions the court held in the case of Sakal Papers Ltd. Vs. Union of India that restraint on the extent to publish any number of pages or to circulate it to any number of persons, was a direct infringement of the right to freedom of speech and expression.

'Without liberty of circulation, the publication would be of no value.' The Court further laid down that the court must be ever vigilant in guarding perhaps the most precious of all the freedoms guaranteed by our Constitution.

The freedom of speech and expression is of paramount importance under a democratic constitution which envisages changes in the composition of legislatures and governments and must be preserved.

In the Banett Coleman & Co. Ltd. case, the Court observed that the individual rights of freedom of speech and expression of editors, directors and shareholders are all exercised through their newspapers through which they speak.

But any press reporter will say that he cannot do anything that his boss, proprietors or editors don't like. There are monopolies in the media. They will not allow publishing against their business interests or political interests.

The present day newspaper proprietors do not set much, more store by the famous remark made by C.P. Scott of the Manchester Guardian that 'comment is free, but facts are sacred'. The press should be purveyor of truth. The liberty which is taken with facts in our media makes mockery of the term 'freedom of press'.

The Indian press had discharged the heavy and crucial responsibilities cast upon it, during Indo-Pak War of December, 1971 and Kargil War in 1999. Almost all the newspapers brushing aside their sectional differences and ideological cleavages provided strength to the leadership and rejuvenated national solidarity. So the press is not only the vehicle of 'Vox Populi' but also mobilises the public opinion.

Morbidity of Indian press also owes to the ill-conditioned journalism and the commercialisation of newspapers and television channels through advertisements etc. But apparently it appears that the Indian press enjoys a greater quantum of freedom of expression than press of other Asian democracies. But analysing in proper perspective, our press has been handicapped by the unostensible hands of the proprietors.

It was the duty of the press to bring about awareness among the people of the new changes taking place in the country. It is regretted that the Indian press tended to give undue importance to politics and political bickering. Due attention should be given to economic, social and scientific matters.

RS Sarkaria, ex-chairman of the Press Council expressed that the press people also have frailties; after all they are also human beings. The executives provide facilities like house allotments or sites, free passes, taking journalists on holidays etc. The rural press also enjoys the facilities provided to them by either government machineries or local business or the vested interests to a great extent. This situation should be avoided.

It is a fact that the press enjoys lot of benefits and government patronage through advertisements, supply of paper, newsprint and also by way of postal concessions and the accreditation and foreign travels on government trips.

However, it is regrettable that no such concession to purchase paper on subsidised price is available to magazines which make permanent impact to formulate public opinion unlike availability of newsprint to the newspapers.

At present, the only safety valve against the conduct of press is the Press Council, which is a body made by the press people.

Now, it is functioning well. However, there is a need to have an Ombudsman headed by a retired Supreme Court judge and independent from all corners to hear all parties, that is, press, public and the affected persons and can accordingly give judgment and impose penalty or punishment on the defaulting press. At present, there is thankfully one.

Therefore, inspite of the fact that the Constitution of India guarantees and safeguards freedom of expression, we cannot really say that India has a free press as long as vested interests keep their stranglehold on it. And even when that has been removed, it will be free in the real sense of the term only when it establishes real rapport with the people of India as a whole.

It is a fact that the freedom of press is sometimes misused by newspaper man by publishing tabloid stories regarding personal life of celebrities to increase their circulation or TRP. On many occasions, the Indian press has failed.

For example, in case of Lalu Prasad and his Janata Dal almost all newspapers predicted defeat for Lalu Prasad Yadav in Bihar assembly elections in early 1995 and in 2015. All newspapers almost used to depict him in a funny manner. But the masses of Bihar again voted him and his Janata Dal back to power in an election in which best efforts were made to conduct free and fair elections in Bihar.

Similarly, the Left Front Government in West Bengal didn't bother much about the power of the press. Yet the communists were elected term after terms to capture power in West Bengal for more than thirty years. Unnecessarily, the press indulges in forecasting of political events and repercussions or fallouts which are very uncertain.

The press at the same time develops the vested interest to patronise a few individuals or party/parties which is very harmful for the democracy. By talking 90 percent about 10 percent and 10 percent about 90 percent, the Indian press has created dependency of people upon the politics.

In fact, the people have developed an inherent indulgence in political issues and gimmicks which are uncertain. The Indian press, whether print media or electronic media, gives lot of coverage to crimes like rape and murder, which spoils the mood of readers in the morning.

As a result, the capacity of work of the Indians is adversely affected. It creates lack of faith in the Indian press as general citizens find that the society outside their periphery is not as bad or insecure as projected by the press.

The press should rather be a medium of motivation to the people of India. Therefore, if the Indian press takes leadership in social, economic, educational and cultural issues, it can never fail and will ever shine as truth always shines.

NEED OF THE HOUR

The institution of Ombudsman on the pattern of Lokayukta can cure the ills to a large extent. So far, Press Council as a body is constituted with majority of people connected with the press directly or indirectly. Even some media houses have their own

Ombudsman institution like NDTV, which has the duty of investigating and reporting back to the complainants after necessary action.

Publicity based on impartial inquiry is a powerful lever. However, recent raid by income tax and CBI on the premises of promoter directors of NDTV are being questioned by the veterans of the press but one has to wait and see what finally emerges as truth. If the raid was intended to gag the voice of NDTV, they can subsequently file cases of unwarranted harassment by the authorities or officers personally without justification and claim compensation apart from exposing the government in their sinister motive.

Where a complaint is found to be justified, an Ombudsman can often persuade the Press Council or private press to enforce disciplinary action against the delinquent newspapers, TV channel, editors, reporters, journalists or news manager. He can prevail upon to pay compensation in suitable cases.

Thus, the establishment of proper institution of Ombudsman will create a proper mechanism of public accountability of the press along with its freedom which is very much desirable nowadays.

The Alive, August 2-17

♦♦♦

Bibliography

A. BOOKS

Dr. Agrawal, P.K.
- Psychology of Bureaucrats, Manas Publications, Daryaganj, New Delhi-2, Year 2016, Total Pages 208
- Solution to Naxalism, Manas Publications, Year 2016, Total Pages 152
- Land and Poverty Alleviation, Kalpaz Publications, Satyawati Nagar, Delhi-52, year 2015, Total Pages 260
- Land Reforms in States and Union Territories in India, Concept Publishing Company Pvt. Ltd., New Delhi-59, Year-2010, Total Pages 254
- Land Reforms in India, MD Publications Pvt. Ltd., 11 Darya Ganj, New Delhi-2, Year 1993, Total Pages 272
- Commentary on the Constitution of India, Prabhat Prakashan, Asaf Ali Road, New Delhi-2, Year 2017, Total Pages 496

Row, Joya – Profile of the Perfect Person, published by Jaico Publishing House, Fort, Mumbai-1, Year 2011, Total Pages 139

Sen, Amartya – Inequality Re-examined, Year 1997

Website: – Amazon

Partha Sarathi, A – Bhagwad Gita, published by A Partha Sarathi, 1 A Land Sand, Mumbai-6, Year 2008, Total Pages 868

B. Reports, Law Reporters, Government Publications etc.

All India Reporter Ltd. (AIR), PB-209, Congress Nagar, Nagpur-440012

Supreme Court Cases (SCC), Eastern Book Company, Lal Bagh, Lucknow-1, U.P.

C. Acts, Statutes, Regulations

All India Services (Conduct) Rules, 1968

Black Money Act, 2015

Companies Act, 2013
Commission of Inquiry Act, 1952
Factories Act, 1948
Indian Evidence Act, 1872
Indian Penal Code, 1860
Judges Protection Act, 1985
The Delhi (Right of Citizen to Time Bound Delivery of Services) Act, 2011
The Foreign Exchange Management Act, 1999
The Legal Services Authorities Act, 1987
The Prevention of Corruption Act, 1947 & 1988
The Prevention of Money Laundering Act, 2002
The Lokpal and Lokayutas Act, 2013
The Punjab Right to Service Commission Act
14th Law Commission of India
120th Report of Law Commission of India
154th Report of Law Commission of India
104th Report of Law Commission of India
Money Lenders Act
Sexual Harassment of Women at Work Place (Prevention, Prohibition and Redressal) Act, 2013
Public Records Act
States Reorganization Act, 1956
The United Nations Conventions, 2005
Land Acquisition Act, 2013
NDPS Act
STORFA, 2006
West Bengal Land Reforms Act, 1955
Right to Information Act
The Societies Registration Act, 1860
The Indian Income Tax Act, 1961
Benami Transactions (Prohibition) Act, 2016
Environment Protection Act, 1986
Newspaper (Paper and Page) Act, 1956
Authoritative versions of above Acts or statutes can generally be found from the Central government website: www.legislative.gov.in

◆◆◆

Index

A

B

H

I

J

K

L

M

N

O

P

R

S

T

U

V

W

Y

♦♦♦